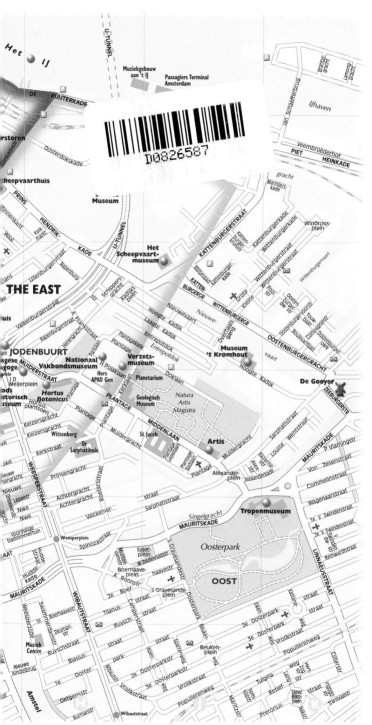

Fodor's

25 Best

AMSTERDAM

How to Use This Book

KEY TO SYMBOLS	
✚ Map reference to the accompanying fold-out map	🖳 Nearest canal boat or ferry stop
✉ Address	♿ Facilities for visitors with disabilities
☎ Telephone number	❓ Other practical information
⊙ Opening/closing times	▷ Further information
🍴 Restaurant or café	ℹ Tourist information
🚆 Nearest rail station	✋ Admission charges: Expensive (over €9), Moderate (€3–€9) and Inexpensive (€2 or less)
Ⓜ Nearest Metro (subway) station	
🚌 Nearest bus or tram route	

This guide is divided into four sections
● Essential Amsterdam: An introduction to the city and tips on making the most of your stay.
● Amsterdam by Area: We've broken the city into five areas, and recommended the best sights, shops, entertainment venues, nightlife and places to eat in each one. Suggested walks help you to explore on foot.
● Where to Stay: The best hotels, whether you're looking for luxury, budget or something in between.
● Need to Know: The info you need to make your trip run smoothly, including getting about by public transport, weather tips, emergency phone numbers and useful websites.

Navigation In the Amsterdam by Area chapter, we've given each area its own colour, which is also used on the locator maps throughout the book and the map on the inside front cover.

Maps The fold-out map accompanying this book is a comprehensive street plan of Amsterdam. The grid on this fold-out map is the same as the grid on the locator maps within the book. We've given grid references within the book for each sight and listing.

Contents

Introducing Amsterdam

How do you define Amsterdam? To some it's canals, carillons ringing out from church steeples and the variety of the Dutch gable. To others it's synonymous with tolerance—of eccentricity, of red light districts and smoking cafés.

Amsterdam is small—you can cross the city centre on foot in 30 minutes—and there are over 800,000 people packed into not quite enough space. Yet the city has so much going on, it will reward you if you visit more than once. It has a changing schedule of special exhibitions, festivals and arts events, from the weirdest avant-garde shows to the works of Rembrandt and Vermeer, which means you are bound to see something different each time. The many faces of Amsterdam help to make it among Europe's most popular destinations.

The city feels like a big village. Amsterdammers' sociability makes it easy to get to know people—as does the fact that many speak several languages. Intellectual, curious about the world and great talkers, Amsterdammers have dared to embark on some of the great social experiments of our time. Prostitution has been tolerated in the city since the 17th century. Amsterdam's liberal drug laws allow licensed cafés to permit the sale of cannabis. The city invented traffic calming—tough laws and schemes to discourage cars but to improve existing driving conditions—and it may yet become the first city to ban cars outright. Gay marriage has been legal in Amsterdam since the beginning of April 2001.

Informality is the norm here. Many local people long ago abandoned formal business attire, and most restaurants are unpretentious. A lot of street corners have a *bruine kroeg* (brown café), named after the mellow hue of the tobacco-stained walls, where people settle down with a newspaper or discuss the issues of the day with friends, which you are welcome to join.

FACTS AND FIGURES

- Bicycles—880,000
- Houseboats—2,500
- Windmills—8
- Canals—165
- Bridges—1,281
- Statues and sculptures—300
- Flower bulbs in parks—600,000
- 16th-, 17th- and 18th-century buildings—8,863

LIFE ON THE WATER

Amsterdam is expanding to handle an expected population of 900,000 by 2020. Most expansion is among what used to be the quays and installations of the old harbour, many of them on artificial islands, along Het IJ waterfront. Cutting-edge architecture is the theme, but space has been kept for refurbished and repurposed warehouses and other buildings.

KING'S DAY

Nothing better sums up Amsterdam than *Koningsdag* (King's Day), the monarch's official birthday (27 April) and the occasion for a citywide street party. Even those Amsterdammers with republican views celebrate. Everyone wears orange, the royal shade, and outdoor concerts are held at the Museumplein, and flea markets pop up all over the city.

CYCLE CITY

Visitors may well be mown down by a speeding bicycle within a few moments of arrival. Designated cycle paths often run contrary to the traffic flow, so look both ways before crossing a road. Join in the fun on a bicycle without brakes—you have to back pedal. Never leave your bicycle unlocked. There are many bicycle rental companies throughout the city.

A Short Stay in Amsterdam

DAY 1

Morning Try to get to the **Anne Frank Huis** (▷ 24–25) when it opens at 9am, to avoid crowds. The experience can leave quite an impression on visitors; afterwards a quiet canal stroll may be the order of the day. Make your way south down to the area of the **Jordaan** (▷ 29) known as the Negen Straatjes (Nine Streets), which straddle the canals from Singel to Prinsengracht. This district is full of interesting, idiosyncratic shops.

Mid-morning Take a break on Huidenstraat at **Pompadour** (▷ 36), a chocolatier and tiny tea shop. After wandering around here for while, make your way up to the pedestrianized Dam, the ceremonial and political heart of the city, dominated by the **Royal Palace** (▷ 45). The square is generally crowded and full of street entertainers.

Lunch On the northern side of Dam is the city's biggest department store, **De Bijenkorf** (▷ 55). You can get a tasty meal at the store's buffet-style restaurant, **Kitchen** (▷ 62), which offers a wide variety at a good price.

Afternoon After lunch, board a canal boat from the jetty on Damrak, near Centraal Station. For about an hour you can cruise around the canal ring, take photographs and listen to a commentary in several languages.

Early evening Most people are curious to see the **Red Light District** (▷ 49) and a visit just before dinner is probably the best time to do this. If you have any reservations about going, keep to the main drag, avoiding side alleys, and you should feel quite at ease.

Dinner For a chic French meal try Michelin-starred **Bridges** (▷ 61) in the Grand hotel on Oudezijds Voorburgwal. For a less expensive, Japanese option go to **Morita-Ya** (▷ 63) on Zeedijk.

DAY 2

Morning Start early at the **Rijksmuseum** (▷ 85), to give yourself time to view as much as you can, and don't miss Rembrandt's famous *Night Watch*. For modern art, go on to the nearby **Van Gogh Museum** (▷ 88–89) to view the works of the master, but expect crowds, especially gathered around the Sunflowers. For those with an interest in drink rather than art, make a detour to visit the **Heineken Experience** (▷ 90) on Stadhouderskade.

Mid-morning Take a break for coffee in the Van Gogh Museum before completing your tour of the masterpieces. Then go down to **Vondelpark** (▷ 87) for a breath of fresh air and a stroll in the park.

Lunch Take lunch at the **Groot Melkhuis** (▷ 94) in the park. If the weather is fine, an outdoor table is a great place for people-watching.

Afternoon The park is the preferred green space of Amsterdammers and a popular place for joggers and walkers. With its 47 hectares (116 acres), it offers a welcome break from the hectic city life. Leave the park by the north end to walk to the smartest shopping street in the city, P.C. Hooftstraat. Here you will find international names as well as local Dutch designers. After some window-shopping or serious spending it's time for dinner.

Dinner Have an early-evening meal at **Brasserie Keyzer** (▷ 94) where musicians and concertgoers have been dining since 1900.

Evening Go next door to the magnificent **Concertgebouw** (▷ 92) for an evening of classical music or throw caution to the wind with a flutter at **Holland Casino Amsterdam** (▷ 93).

Top 25 Sights

► ► ►

Amsterdam Museum
▷ 40–41 The place to familiarize yourself with city history.

Anne Frank Huis
▷ 24–25 The young Jewish diarist's wartime refuge is sad yet inspiring.

Begijnhof ▷ 42 A haven of spiritual tranquillity and unhurried peace in the heart of the city.

Woonbootmuseum
▷ 28 Although a museum, this canal barge still feels like someone's home.

Westerkerk ▷ 27 Climb to the top of the tower for some great views across the city.

Vondelpark ▷ 87 This park throbs with life on a warm summer's day—a great place for people-watching.

Van Gogh Museum
▷ 88–89 You'll have to join the line to see the Sunflowers at this huge collection of Van Gogh's work.

Tropenmuseum ▷ 98 The vivid, vibrant story of daily life in the tropics is told in this extraordinary museum.

Stedelijk Museum ▷ 86 This must for modern art lovers features works by Mondrian, Picasso, Warhol and many others.

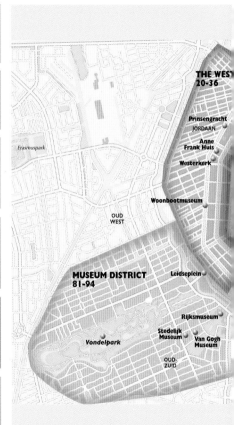

Singel ▷ 50 Take a boat trip along the canal for the best view of the city and learn about its history.

Rosse Buurt ▷ 49 Most people just can't resist a look at the brazen Red Light District.

Rijksmuseum ▷ 85 The showcase of the artist Rembrandt and wonderful 17th-century Dutch art.

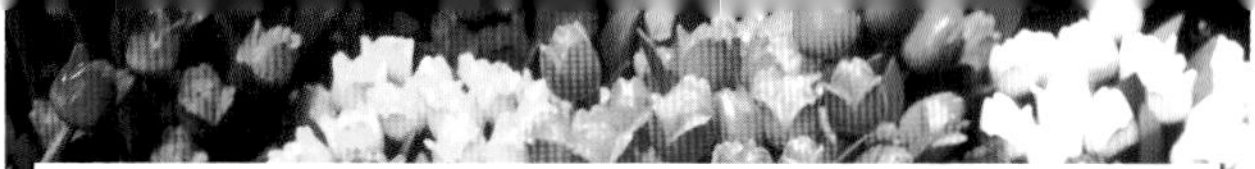

These pages are a quick guide to the Top 25, which are described in more detail later. Here they are listed alphabetically and the tinted background shows the area they are in.

CENTRAL AMSTERDAM
37–64

Herengracht
Singel
Nieuwe Kerk
CENTRUM
Koninklijk Paleis
Ons' Lieve Heer op Solder
Oude Kerk
CHINATOWN
Rosse Buurt
NEMO Science Museum
Oosterdok
Het IJ
IJhaven

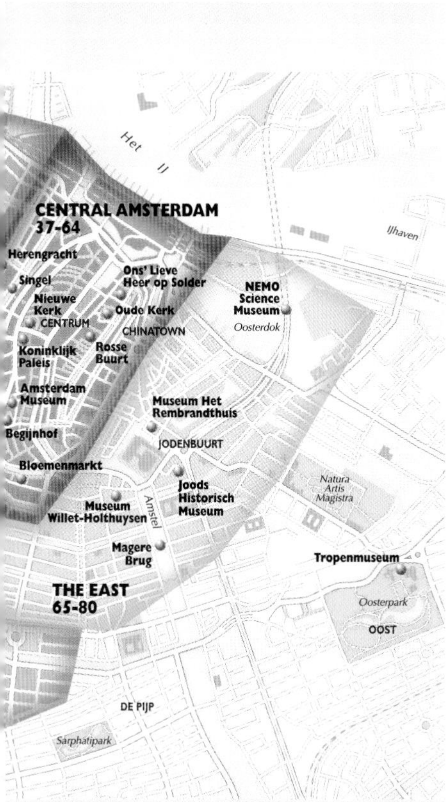

Amsterdam Museum
Begijnhof
Museum Het Rembrandthuis
JODENBUURT
Bloemenmarkt
Museum Willet-Holthuysen
Joods Historisch Museum
Amstel
Natura Artis Magistra
Magere Brug
Tropenmuseum
THE EAST
65–80
Oosterpark
OOST
DE PIJP
Sarphatipark

Shopping

Amsterdam is full of fascinating shops that specialize in everything from toothbrushes to aboriginal art, children's comics to art deco lamps, potted plants to exotic cut flowers, and liquorice to cheese.

Off the Beaten Track
These character-rich shops are not always in the obvious places. Amsterdam's main shopping streets—Nieuwendijk and Kalverstraat—are dominated by global brands. Instead you need to look where the city rents are lower: along Haarlemmerstraat, Damstraat and in the cross streets of the Canal Circle and the Jordaan. These cross streets were deliberately zoned for commercial use in the 17th century, when the canal circle was planned, and thrived on the trade in furs and hides. Just go and wander down Reestraat, Hartenstraat, Berenstraat, Runstraat and Huidenstraat to find a medley of small specialist shops, cafés and art galleries, which have replaced the original furriers.

Individualists
The entrepreneurs who run these shops have a real passion for their products and they want to share their enthusiasm, so customers are not treated merely as consumers, but as fellow connoisseurs. Some will spend all day talking to you about their sources and stock. Others are busy making the products they sell, such as gorgeously decorated hats, Venetian-style masks, recycled vintage clothing, evening dresses or costume jewellery.

Clogs, flowers and Delftware are great gifts to bring home

CLOMPING CLOGS

Think Amsterdam and you'll probably think of clogs—or *klompen* as they are known in Dutch—a splendidly onomatopoeic word that imitates the heavy clomping sound the wooden shoes make as they hit the city's pavements. They are carved from a single block of poplar wood and are extremely comfortable. Most, however, are sold as decorative souvenirs rather than as footwear. You'll find them painted with windmills, tulips or cheeses.

Shopping with a Difference

The range of specialties is incredible. For lovers of chocolate, try Pompadour (▷ 36). Feeling guilty about consuming all that sugar? De Witte Tandenwinkel (The White Teeth Shop ▷ 33) sells every imaginable style of toothbrush and every possible type of toothpaste. Olivaria (Hazenstraat 2A, tel 638 3552) is devoted to olive oil. Joe's Vliegerwinkel (Nieuwe Hoogstraat 19, tel 625 0139) sells only toys that fly—bright kites, boomerangs and frisbees. Lovers of children's and adults' comics, new and second-hand, should visit Lambiek (▷ 57). Clogs are synonymous with the Netherlands, so for a selection check out De Klompenboer (▷ 78). Rare and beautiful 19th-century accessories for both men and women can be found at 1953 Retro & Chic (Staalstraat 2, tel 493 3582).

Blooming Wonderful

You will find more flowers and bulbs in Amsterdam than in any other European city— not just in the floating flower market, but all around the Canal Circle. A bouquet of blooms— always buy blooms that are still closed—or a packet of bulbs make a great souvenir of your stay, but be sure to check the import regulations first.

FLEA MARKETS

The dark days of World War II engendered a habit of thrift in the citizens of Amsterdam, and even in today's prosperous times, no true Amsterdammer ever throws anything away. Instead, everything—from old light bulbs to ancient newspapers—gets recycled at one of the city's flea markets. The biggest and best known is the one on two sides of the Stadhuis (Town Hall) on Waterlooplein. Stalls here mix the new, the old and the unimaginably decrepit. Pick up very serviceable second-hand clothes, craft items and jewellery, and wonder why anyone would want to buy a broken radio, chipped vase or a doll without a head. Other flea markets include the Antiekcentrum Amsterdam and the market at Noordermarkt.

Museum shops are a good source of souvenirs from the city. Cheese and plants are popular, too

Shopping by Theme

Whether you're looking for a department store, a quirky boutique, or something in between, you'll find it all in Amsterdam. On this page shops are listed by theme. For a more detailed write-up, see the individual listings in Amsterdam by Area.

Art and Antiques
Amsterdam Vintage Watches (▷ 55)
Antiekcentrum Amsterdam (▷ 32)
Gastronomie Nostalgie (▷ 56)
Jaski Gallery (▷ 78)
Kramer Kunst & Antiek (▷ 78)
Rembrandt Art Market (▷ 78)

Books
American Book Center (▷ 55)
Architectura & Natura (▷ 55)
The Book Exchange (▷ 55)
De Kinderboekwinkel (▷ 33)
Scheltema (▷ 58)

Dutch Souvenirs
Bonebakker (▷ 92)
Dam Square Souvenirs (▷ 56)
Galleria d'Arte Rinascimento (▷ 32)
Het Oud-Hollandsch Snoepwinkeltje (▷ 32)
Jorrit Heinen (▷ 32)

Fashion
byAMFI (▷ 55)
Good Genes (▷ 92)
Oqium (▷ 57)
SPRMRKT (▷ 33)
Tenue de Nîmes (▷ 33)

Food and Drink
De Bierkoning (▷ 55)
Het Hanzen Huis (▷ 56)
H.P. de Vreng and Zonen (▷ 56)
KOKO Coffee & Design (▷ 57)
Jordino (▷ 32)
Patisserie Holtkamp (▷ 78)
Pompadour (▷ 36)

Specialist Shops
Atelier Tempel (▷ 104)
Azarius (▷ 32)
Blender (▷ 92)
BLGK Edelsmeden (▷ 32)
Concerto (▷ 78)
Condomerie (▷ 55)
Droog (▷ 56)
Frozen Fountain (▷ 32)
Gassan Diamonds (▷ 78)
Gathershop (▷ 104)
Gone with the Wind (▷ 78)
The Headshop (▷ 56)

Hempshopper (▷ 56)
Hutspot (▷ 32)
Jacob Hooy (▷ 57)
Juffrouw Splinter (▷ 32)
Kitsch Kitchen (▷ 33)
De Klompenboer (▷ 78)
Lambiek (▷ 57)
Mechanisch Speelgoed (▷ 33)
Mint Mini Mall (▷ 33)
P.G.C. Hajenius (▷ 57)
Pols Potten (▷ 104)
La Savonnerie (▷ 33)
Shirdak (▷ 33)
Terra Incognita (▷ 92)
Webers Holland (▷ 58)
De Witte Tandenwinkel (▷ 33)
WonderWood (▷ 58)

Stores, Malls and Markets
Amstelveld Plantenmarkt (▷ 78)
De Bazaar (▷ 104)
De Bijenkorf (▷ 55)
Dun Yong (▷ 56)
Kalvertoren (▷ 57)
Magna Plaza (▷ 57)
Waterloopleinmarkt (▷ 78)

Amsterdam by Night

Amsterdam is one of Europe's most vibrant nightlife capitals. On a mild summer's evening nothing beats just walking by the canal, or gliding along the canals in a glass-topped boat, to see the historic bridges and buildings spotlighted in white lights.

Your Kind of Music

There is always something going on in the classical music world, most of it at the Concertgebouw (▷ 92–93) and the Beurs van Berlage (▷ 59). In addition, many churches host choral concerts and organ recitals, the Melkweg and Paradiso nightclubs (▷ 93) have rock and pop, Jazz Café Alto (▷ 34) has jazz and blues, the Muziekgebouw aan 't IJ (▷ 105) has experimental music, and live-music venue Bourbon Street (▷ 34) has a bit of everything.

Out on the Town

The city's clubs offer all kinds of entertainment, including plenty that is explicitly erotic in the Red Light District with its sex shows and somewhat sleazy bars. Rembrandtplein throngs with pre-party drinkers. They are likely to head for Escape (▷ 79) or the more sophisticated De Kroon (▷ 79) and Café Schiller (▷ 79). Leidseplein is another popular spot, with its lively street cafés and bars.

Something to Watch

There is plenty going on at the cinemas, both mainstream and art house. Don't miss the Pathé Tuschinski (▷ 60) in a splendid art deco building.

Take a stroll through the city at night—the lights brighten up the canals, bridges and buildings

CITY OF JAZZ

This is a city that adores jazz and blues, and there are scores of venues to choose from, including the legendary Bimhuis at the Muziekgebouw aan 't IJ and Jazz Café Alto. However, Amsterdam cedes to Rotterdam the privilege of hosting the renowned North Sea Jazz Festival, which takes place in mid-July (northseajazz.com) and attracts big international stars.

Where to Eat

Choice is the key when eating out in Amsterdam. There is a great selection of fusion cooking, a wide variety of tastes and a good range of prices.

Global Cuisine
Centuries of colonialism and a multicultural population are reflected in the city's cuisine. The most common of the ethnic cuisines are Indonesian and Chinese. Dutch colonists added their own dishes to the basic Indonesian meal, and most popular is the *rijsttafel,* which literally means rice table. With rice as the focal point, there can be anything from 15 to 30 dishes to accompany it. For more traditional Dutch food there are small intimate restaurants serving authentic cuisine. There is, however, a trend toward less heavy fare, a New Dutch cooking, which is going from strength to strength.

Keeping the Price Down
If you are on a budget try the *eetcafés,* in which traditional Dutch food or stylish contemporary dishes are served. You could try the *dagschotel* (dish of the day) or the *dagmenu* (menu of the day).

Practical Tips
Always reserve in advance for that special treat, as restaurants tend to be small and fill up quickly. The Dutch like to eat early, between 6.30 to 8, so restaurants are busier at this time. Eating out is a laid-back, casual affair and a dress code only applies to the smartest of luxury and hotel restaurants.

From top: Pendergast; Vinkeles Restaurant at Hotel Dylan; Visaandeschelde; Ciel Bleu Restaurant

AUTHENTIC DUTCH CUISINE

The most delicious dishes include *erwtensoep* (thick split-pea soup), *stamppot* (mashed potatoes mixed with vegetables, served with meat and gravy), *gerookte paling* (smoked eel), *haring* (raw herring), *pannekoeken* (sweet and tasty pancakes), *stroopwafels* (waffles) and cheeses. *Kroketten, bitterballen* (both a type of croquette), and fries served with mayonnaise are also Dutch classics.

Where to Eat by Cuisine

There are plenty of places to eat to suit all tastes and budgets in Amsterdam. On this page they are listed by cuisine. For a more detailed description of each restaurant, see Amsterdam by Area.

Cafés
1e Klas (▷ 60)
Café Americain (▷ 94)
Café Bern (▷ 61)
Café Duende (▷ 35)
Café Loetje (▷ 94)
Café Luxembourg (▷ 61)
Pendergast (▷ 106)
Rose's Cantina (▷ 63)
Van Puffelen (▷ 36)

Dutch
De Blauwe Hollander
   (▷ 35)
Brasserie Keyzer (▷ 94)
Café-Restaurant
   Amsterdam (▷ 106)
Choux (▷ 80)
Haesje Claes (▷ 62)
In de Waag (▷ 62)
Maximiliaan (▷ 63)
Moeders (▷ 35)
Tomaz (▷ 64)

East Asian
Geisha (▷ 61)
Morita-Ya (▷ 63)
Norling Restaurant
   (▷ 63)
Thaise Snackbar Bird
   (▷ 64)
Wok to Walk (▷ 64)

Elegant Dining
De Belhamel (▷ 35)
Bord'Eau (▷ 60)
Bridges (▷ 61)
Ciel Bleu (▷ 106)

De Gouden Reael
   (▷ 106)
Restaurant De Kas
   (▷ 106)
La Rive (▷ 106)
De Silveren Spiegel
   (▷ 63)
D'Vijff Vlieghen (▷ 64)
Vinkeles (▷ 36)

Fish
Pesca (▷ 36)
The Seafood Bar (▷ 94)
Visaandeschelde
   (▷ 106)

French
Breitner (▷ 80)
Chez Georges (▷ 61)

Indonesian
Aneka Rasa (▷ 60)
Indrapura (▷ 80)
Kantjil & de Tiger (▷ 62)
Tempo Doeloe (▷ 80)

Italian
La Perla (▷ 35)
Segugio (▷ 80)
Toscanini (▷ 36)

Snacks and Eetcafés
Baton Brasserie (▷ 35)
Café de Fles (▷ 80)
Foodhallen (▷ 94)
Gartine (▷ 61)
Greenwood's (▷ 62)
Groot Melkhuis (▷ 94)

Kitchen (▷ 62)
Kwekkeboom (▷ 62)
Pannenkoekenhuis
   Upstairs (▷ 63)
Piqniq (▷ 36)
La Place (▷ 80)
Pompadour (▷ 36)
Toastable (▷ 64)
van Kerkwijk (▷ 64)
Winkel 43 (▷ 36)

Vegetarian
Bloem (▷ 80)
De Bolhoed (▷ 35)
Latei (▷ 63)
Semhar (▷ 36)

Top Tips For...

These great suggestions will help you tailor your ideal visit to Amsterdam, no matter how you choose to spend your time. Each suggestion has a fuller write-up elsewhere in the book.

A DUTCH MEMENTO

Tulips from Amsterdam and many other flowers and plants from the Bloemenmarkt (▷ 43).
For salty black liquorice go to Het Oud-Hollandsch Snoepwinkeltje (▷ 32).
Handpainted Delftware plates, vases and more will be found at Jorrit Heinen (▷ 32).

SHOPS WITH CHARACTER

If you like the retro look for your home, go to Juffrouw Splinter (▷ 32) or WonderWood (▷ 58).
Everything made of hemp? It's true at Hempshopper (▷ 56).
Herbs, spices and homeopathic remedies are on sale in this old-fashioned 1743 apothecary, Jacob Hooy (▷ 57).

Look out for Delftware on sale (above); sampling Dutch cuisine, and the pretty Skinny Bridge (below)

HONEST DUTCH FARE

Try typical Dutch snacks such as *bitterballen*, *loempias*, *kroketten* and others at Winkel 43 (▷ 36).
Robust home cooking can be found at De Blauwe Hollander (▷ 35). You are guaranteed huge portions.
D'Vijff Vlieghen (▷ 64) brings a more modern, lighter touch to the sometimes heavy traditional Dutch food.

PHOTO OPS

At night, vist the illuminated Magere Brug (Skinny Bridge, ▷ 69) for portraits.
The Openbare Bibliotheek has a top-floor cafeteria and terrace (▷ 80) with a panoramic view of the city.
Take a tour up the steeple of the Westerkerk (▷ 27) and get a neighbourhood perspective from above.

Go for a walk along the canal bank or stroll in one of the parks

A ROOM WITH A VIEW

Stay at Hotel Estheréa (▷ 110) for a perfectly placed quiet spot overlooking the Singel (▷ 50).

More river view than canal, but the opulent De L'Europe (▷ 112) has a great position.

Located on the peaceful Keizersgracht, is the charming Canal House hotel (▷ 110).

THE LIVE MUSIC SCENE

Don't miss the world-famous Concertgebouw (▷ 92) for excellent classical music.

For the very best in live jazz and blues stroll down to Jazz Café Alto (▷ 34).

For rock to reggae, Amsterdam's best live music is at Paradiso (▷ 93).

AMSTERDAM ON A SHOESTRING

The world-renowned Concertgebouw was built in 1888 and designed by A.L. van Gendt (above)

You can't beat the central location for the price at the Hotel Prinsenhof (▷ 109).

Kitchen (▷ 62) in De Bijenkorf department store (▷ 55) offers good value for money and a good view, too.

If you intend to use public transportation a lot in a day or over several days, buy one-day or multi-day tickets (▷ 118–119).

GOING OUT AND ABOUT

You can't go to Amsterdam without going on a canal cruise, by day or night (▷ 118, 119).

Walk, jog, skate or run around the Vondelpark (▷ 87), the city's favourite green space.

Rent a bike (▷ 119) and join the locals for the best way to get around the city.

Amsterdam is famous for its bikes

STYLISH LIVING

If you like boutique hotels with oodles of
style, you will love the Dylan (▷ 112).
Classical chic at the De Belhamel (▷ 35),
serving high-class French cuisine.
Take a tour around Coster Diamonds
(▷ 90) and then choose your jewel.

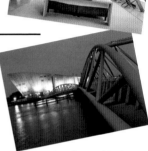

ENTERTAINING THE KIDS

Take the Hop On-Hop Off boat tour
out to the copper-clad, hands-on
NEMO Science Museum (▷ 72–73).
Spend the morning, rain or shine, at
Artis (▷ 100), one of the oldest zoos in
Europe.
Kids will be thrilled with The
Amsterdam Dungeon (▷ 51), featuring
interactive live actor shows.

*The Dylan Hotel (top);
the stunning building of
the NEMO (above)*

QUIRKY MUSEUMS

The Amsterdam Tulip Museum (▷ 29)
is the only museum in the world to be
dedicated to Holland's ubiquitous flower.
Discover all about life aboard in the
quaint Woonbootmuseum (▷ 28).
The unusual Tropenmuseum (▷ 98)
has evocative displays from around
the world.

THE BEST CANALS

Herengracht (▷ 44)—if you take a boat trip
you will go along here, but it's also great to
walk beside.
Singel (▷ 50)—wider than most but there is
lots of interest along its banks.
Prinsengracht (▷ 26)—check out the vibrant
houseboats and the merchants' houses.

*The elaborate interior of the Tropenmuseum
(right); take a trip to the Artis zoo
with the kids (above)*

The western area of Amsterdam is where
the real soul of the city resides. This is very
much a local neighbourhood, with beautiful canals, lovely old houses and individual
shops, making it very photogenic.

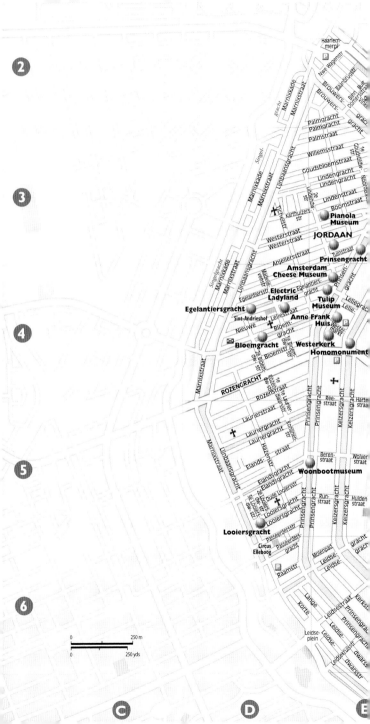

Haarlem-
merpl·

Nwe Wagenstr

Brouwers-

Brouwers·

Marnixkade

Marnixstraat

gracht

Barndusstr

Domenisgracht

Palmgracht

Palmgracht

Palmstraat

gracht

Willemsstraat

Goudsbloemstraat

Goudsbloem

Noordern·

Lindengracht

Lindengracht

Lindenstraat

Boomstraat

**Pianola
Museum**

Marnixkade

Marnixstraat

Lijnbaansgracht

karthuizers

Tichelstr

str

Westerstraat

Westerstraat

JORDAAN

Tuinstraat

Singel-gracht

Singel

Anjeliersstraat

Prinsengracht

Marnixkade

Marnixstraat

Madelie·
verstr

Egelantiersstr

**Amsterdam
Cheese Museum**

Egelantiers·
gracht

Prinsen·

gracht

**Electric
Ladyland**

**Tulip
Museum**

Lelie

Leliegrac

Egelantiersgracht

Sint-Andrieshof

Leliestraat

**Anne Frank
Huis**

Wester

Nieuwe

Bloem·
gracht

markt

Bloemgracht

Bloemstr

ge bloem

dw. str

2e bloem

Westerkerk

Homomonument

Marnixstraat

ROZENGRACHT

1e rozen

Rozengracht

2e laurier

3e laurier

1e laurier

Prinsengracht

Prinsengracht

Ree·
straat

Keizersgracht

Keizersgracht

Harte
straa

Laurierstraat

Lauriergracht

Lauriergracht

Marnixstraat

Lijnbaansgracht

Elands·

Hazenstr

straat

Beren-
straat

Wolver
straat

Elandsgracht

Elandsgracht

Oude Looiersstr

Woonbootmuseum

Prinsengracht

Prinsengracht

Run-
straat

Keizersgracht

Keizersgracht

Hulden
straat

3e Looier

Looiersgracht

Looiersgracht

Passeerdersstr

Looiersgracht

Passeerders·
gracht

gracht

Keizers·

**Circus
Elleboog**

Raamstr

Molenpad

Leidse·

Leidse·

gracht

grach

Lange

Korte

Leidsestraat

Prinsengracht

kerkstr

Prinsengrac

Leidse·
plein

Leidse·

Leidse·

Leidsekruisstr

dwarsstr

dwsstr

2

3

4

5

6

0   250 m

0   250 yds

C   D   E

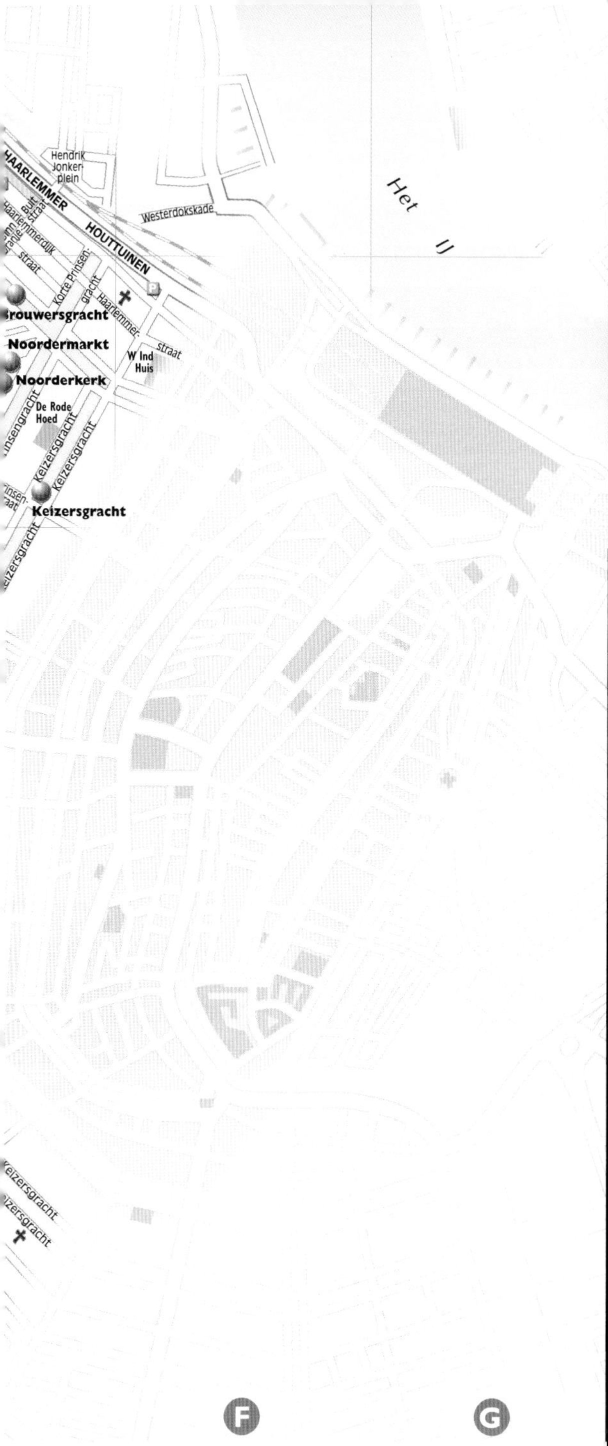
Hendrik Jonker-plein
HAARLEMMER HOUTTUINEN
Westerdokskade
Het IJ
Buiten Oranje-straat
Haarlemmerdijk
Korte Prinsen-gracht
Haarlemmer-straat
Brouwersgracht
Noordermarkt
W Ind Huis
Noorderkerk
De Rode Hoed
Prinsengracht
Keizersgracht
Keizersgracht
Keizersgracht
F
G

Anne Frank Huis

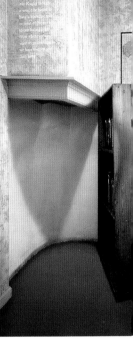

DID YOU KNOW?

● The Nazis occupied Amsterdam for five years.
● Of Holland's 140,000 pre-war Jewish population only 28,000 survived.

TIPS

● The experience of visiting can be distressing—leave time to come to terms with what you have seen.
● An online ticket for a specific timeslot is required for visiting between 9am and 3.30pm. After this time, a ticket can be purchased at the museum entrance.

"My greatest wish is to be a journalist, and later on, a famous writer…I'd like to publish a book called *The Secret Annexe*. It remains to be seen whether I'll succeed, but my diary can serve as a basis."

Unfulfilled wish Anne Frank wrote these words in her diary on Thursday 11 May 1944, just under three months before she was captured by the Nazis. She never saw them published, but instead died in the concentration camp at Bergen-Belsen at age 15.

The Secret Annexe After Nazi Germany invaded the Netherlands in 1940, increasingly severe anti-Semitic measures were introduced. In 1942, the Frank and Van Pels (Van Daan) families, and Fritz Pfeffer (Alfred Dussel) went

Clockwise from left: a display inside Anne Frank Huis; the bookcase that hid the secrect entrance where Anne and her family hid from the Nazis in 1942 for two years; the exterior of the building; Anne's passport picture from 1942

into hiding. For the next two years, Anne Frank kept a diary describing daily life and the families' fear of discovery—until they were betrayed to the Nazis in 1944. Her father was the only one of the group to survive. In 1947, following her wishes, he published her diary, calling it *Het Achterhuis (The Secret Annexe)*.

Anne's legacy More than one million visitors annually make their way through the revolving bookcase that conceals the entrance to the small, gloomy rooms so vividly described in the diary. Pencil lines chart the children's growth. The building is preserved by the Anne Frank Foundation, founded to combat racism and anti-Semitism. In one entry, Anne wrote: "I want to go on living even after my death!" Thanks to her diary, this wish, at least, came true.

THE BASICS

annefrank.org

➕ E4

✉ Prinsengracht 263–267

☎ 556 7105

🕐 Apr–Oct daily 9am–10pm; Nov–Mar daily 9am–7pm (Sat until 9pm)

🚋 Tram 13, 14, 17. Hop On-Hop Off bus stop 11

🚌 Hop On-Hop Off stop 6

♿ Partial

✋ Moderate

❓ 30-min introductory film

Prinsengracht

The handsome Prince's Canal with its attractive buildings

THE BASICS

➕ E3
🍴 Bars, cafés, restaurants
🚊 Tram 1, 2, 4, 5, 6, 13, 14, 16, 17. Hop On-Hop Off bus stop 11
🚢 Hop On-Hop Off stop 6

HIGHLIGHTS

● Amstelkerk (▷ 75)
● Anne Frank Huis (▷ 24–25)
● Noorderkerk (▷ 30)
● Noordermarkt (▷ 30)
● Westerkerk (▷ 27)

DID YOU KNOW?

● Prinsengracht is 4.5km (3 miles) long, 2m (6ft) deep and 25m (80ft) wide to accommodate four lanes of shipping.
● A law (dating from 1565) restricts the lean of canal houses to 1:25.

Of the three canals that form the Grachtengordel (Canal Ring), Prinsengracht is in many ways the most atmospheric, with its fine merchants' homes, converted warehouses and flower-laden houseboats.

Prince William's canal Prinsengracht (Prince's Canal), named after William of Orange, was dug at the same time as Herengracht and Keizersgracht as part of a massive 17th-century expansion scheme. Together these three form the city's distinctive horseshoe-shaped Grachtengordel (Canal Ring). Less exclusive than the other two waterways, with smaller houses, Prinsengracht became an important thoroughfare lined with warehouses and merchants' homes. Cargo would be unloaded from ships into fourth-floor storehouses by means of the massive hoist-beams seen today on the gables of many buildings (and still used for lifting furniture). Some houses were built with a deliberate tilt, to protect their facades from the goods as they were hoisted.

Floating homes Today, you'll also see some of Amsterdam's most beautiful houseboats, some with gardens, moored along Prinsengracht, near Brouwersgracht and alongside the ivy-covered quays close to the Amstel. Amsterdammers have long lived on houseboats, but the housing crisis after World War II caused the population of boat-people to rocket, and there are more than 2,500 legal houseboats in Amsterdam.

The church's tower with a stunning crown (left); a view along Prince's Canal (right)

Westerkerk

This is the most beautiful of the four churches built in the 17th century to the north, south, east and west of the city's centre. The views from the tall tower are superb and make the climb worthwhile.

Masterwork The Amsterdam church most visited by tourists has the largest nave of any Dutch Protestant church, and the tallest tower and largest congregation in the city. It is the masterwork of Dutch architect Hendrick de Keyser, who died in 1621, one year after construction began. Designed to serve the wealthy bourgeoisie living in the new mansions of the Grachtengordel (Canal Ring), it was eventually completed by his son Pieter with Cornelis Dancker in 1631. To its 85m (280ft) tower they added the golden crown—a symbol of the city granted by Habsburg Emperor Maximilian. The views over the Prinsengracht gables can be seen from the tower, popularly called Lange Jan (Tall John). Outside the church, people often lay wreaths at the foot of the statue of Anne Frank, who used to listen to the church carillon while she was in hiding.

Interior The simple, whitewashed interior is laid out in the shape of a double Greek cross. The organ is decorated with musical instruments and frescoes by Gerard de Lairesse, one of Rembrandt's pupils. Rembrandt himself was buried here (in an unknown location) on 8 October 1669, as was his son, Titus, a year earlier in 1668.

THE BASICS

westerkerk.nl
🔲 E4
✉ Prinsengracht 281, Westermarkt
☎ Church 624 7766, tower 612 6856
🕐 Church Mon–Fri 10–5, Sat 11–3; tower Apr–Sep Mon–Fri 10–5. Times vary and church may be closed at times stated
🚊 Tram 13, 14, 17. Hop On-Hop Off bus stop 11
🚢 Hop On-Hop Off stop 6
♿ Few
💷 Church free; tower moderate
❓ Carillon concerts most Tue at noon

HIGHLIGHTS

● Climbing the tower
● Organ, Johannes Duyschot (1686)
● Anne Frank statue, Mari Andriessen
● Rembrandt memorial column
● Grave of Rembrandt's son

Woonbootmuseum

TOP 25

Once a working barge, this museum gives an insight into living on the water

THE BASICS

houseboatmuseum.nl

✚ D5

✉ Prinsengracht opposite No. 296, facing Elandsgracht

☎ 427 0750

🕐 Sep–Jun Tue–Sun 10–5; Jul–Aug daily 10–5

🍴 Café

🚊 Tram 7, 10, 13, 14, 17. Hop On-Hop Off bus stop 11

♿ None

💶 Moderate

HIGHLIGHTS

● Browse the houseboat library
● Watch the slide show
● Sip coffee in the café corner at the same eye level as the ducks

More than 2,500 houseboats line the canals of Amsterdam, homes to people who prefer a life on the water. The Houseboat Museum explores the appeal of a floating home.

Home from home This museum feels exactly like someone's home, and the question that visitors most often ask is whether somebody still lives aboard the *Hendrika Maria*, a retired canal barge built in 1914. In fact, nobody does, but visitors are invited to pretend that they do. In this museum you are allowed to make yourself at home, sit in the comfortable armchairs and browse the books that line the walls of the surprisingly spacious living area.

High maintenance Another common reaction is "I'd love to live on a boat like this". The museum provides plenty of information about houseboat living to encourage such dreams but warns about the rising price of moorings in Amsterdam. The slide show makes it clear that maintaining a houseboat is a work of love. Every three to four years the boat has to be taken out of the water and pressure-hosed to remove corrosive accretions. Loose rivets have to be replaced, along with whole sections of hull if they become thin.

Rising costs When all the costs are added up, houseboat living is not substantially cheaper than living in an equivalent-size apartment. But house-boaters won't be leaving any time soon.

More to See

AMSTERDAM CHEESE MUSEUM

cheesemuseumamsterdam.com

This is more of a cheese shop than an actual museum, but there are some artifacts on display and the chance to dress up as a traditional Dutch cheese farmer. Free cheese tastings are offered.

➕ E4 ✉ Prinsengracht 112 ☎ 331 6605 ⏰ Daily 9–9 🚊 Tram 13, 14, 17 🎫 Free

AMSTERDAM TULIP MUSEUM

amsterdamtulipmuseum.com

This excellent little museum, right next to the Cheese Museum, traces the history of the tulip from its origins in Central Asia. Round off your visit in the shop, which sells every variety of bulb imaginable.

➕ E4 ✉ Prinsengracht 112 ☎ 421 0095 ⏰ Daily 10–6 🚊 Tram 13, 14, 17. Hop On-Hop Off bus stop 11 🎫 Moderate

BLOEMGRACHT AND EGELANTIERSGRACHT

These are narrow canals in the Jordaan, a retreat from the city bustle, and lined with pretty boats.

Amsterdam is renowned for its tulips

➕ D4 🚊 Tram 13, 14, 17. Hop On-Hop Off bus stop 11

BROUWERSGRACHT

Stretching from the Canal Ring into the Jordaan, Brouwersgracht owes its name to the many breweries set up here in the 16th and 17th centuries. Houseboats and the old converted warehouses make this leafy canal particularly photogenic.

➕ E3 🚊 Tram 1, 2, 5, 13, 17. Hop On-Hop Off bus stop 11

ELECTRIC LADYLAND

electric-lady-land.com

Dedicated to fluorescent art, this unique little museum is the only one of its kind in the world.

➕ D4 ✉ Tweede Leliedwarsstraat 5 ☎ 420 3776 ⏰ Tue–Sat 1–6 🚊 Tram 13, 14, 17 🎫 Moderate

HOMOMONUMENT

homomonument.nl

An arresting sculpture, the *Homomonument* (1987) is by Dutch artist Karin Daan. Consisting of three pink granite triangles, the sign gay people were forced to wear during the Nazi occupation, it commemorates all those who have been persecuted because of their sexuality.

➕ E4 ✉ Corner of Westermarkt and Keizersgracht 🚊 Tram 13, 14, 17

JORDAAN

This popular bohemian quarter with its labyrinth of picturesque canals, narrow streets, shops, cafés and restaurants was once a boggy meadow alongside Prinsengracht.

➕ E3 🚊 Tram 3, 10, 13, 14, 17. Hop On-Hop Off bus stop 11

KEIZERSGRACHT

Together with Prinsengracht and Herengracht, this broad and elegant canal, built in 1612 and named Emperor's Canal after Emperor Maximilian I, completes the Grachtengordel (Canal Ring)—the trio of concentric central canals.

🔳 E3 🚋 Tram 1, 2, 5, 13, 14, 16, 17

LOOIERSGRACHT

In the 17th century, the main industry in the Jordaan was tanning, hence the name Tanner's Canal.

🔳 D5 🚋 Tram 7, 10

NOORDERKERK

noorderkerk.org

This austere church, the first in Amsterdam to be constructed in the shape of a Greek cross, was built between 1620 and 1623 for the Protestant workers in the Jordaan area.

🔳 E3 ✉ Noordermarkt 44–48 ☎ 626 6436 🕓 Jul–Aug Sat 10.30–12.30; Sep–Jun Sat and Mon 10.30–12.30 🚋 Tram 1, 2, 5, 13, 14, 17 🎟 Free

NOORDERMARKT

To get a taste of the Jordaan neighbourhood (▷ 29), head for the lively square surrounding the Noorderkerk. Two markets to look out for are the Monday morning Lapjesmarkt textile and second-hand clothing market, and then on Saturday try the Boerenmarkt for organic produce and crafts. It's a good place to assemble a picnic.

🔳 E3 ✉ Noordermarkt 🕓 Mon–Fri 9–1, Sat 9–5 🚋 Tram 1, 2, 5, 13, 17

PIANOLA MUSEUM

pianola.nl

For something completely different visit the small Pianola Museum. A pianola is a mechanized piano and there are nearly 30,000 music rolls in the museum archive. Composers such as Mahler, Debussy, Ravel and Strauss recorded in this way. The museum holds concerts here every month.

🔳 E3 ✉ Westerstraat 106 ☎ 627 9624 🕓 Sun 2–5 🚋 Tram 13, 14, 17. Hop On-Hop Off bus stop 11 🎟 Moderate

Going to market in the Jordaan neighbourhood

A Walk into Jordaan

A pleasant stroll from the busy Dam to the pretty, quiet canals of the west and on through the local district of the Jordaan.

DISTANCE: 4km (2.5 miles) **ALLOW:** 1–2 hours

START

DAM ▦ F4
🚋 Tram 1, 2, 4, 5, 9, 14, 16

END

DAM ▦ F4
🚋 Tram 1, 2, 4, 5, 9, 14, 16

1 Leave Dam via Paleisstraat; continue straight over the scenic Singel, Herengracht and Keizersgracht canals, and then turn right alongside Prinsengracht.

8 Continue across Nieuwezijds Voorburgwal, past the magnificent Nieuwe Kerk (▷ 46) on the left and return to the Dam.

2 Pass Westerkerk (▷ 27) and Anne Frank Huis (▷ 24–25) and turn left on Leliegracht, cross Prinsengracht and double back a few steps along the bank of the canal.

7 Cross by the sluice gates and turn right along the eastern side of Singel, past Amsterdam's narrowest house facade (No. 7). To conclude the walk, turn left at Torensteeg, cross Spui and go along Molensteeg.

3 You will reach the peaceful Bloemgracht (▷ 29) canal. Turn right here, take the second right up Tweede Leliedwarsstraat, cross over Egelantiersgracht (▷ 29) and turn right along its shady bank.

6 You come to attractive Brouwersgracht (▷ 29), lined with traditional barges and houseboats. Cross Brouwersgracht at Herengracht and walk along Brouwersgracht to Singel.

4 Turn left up Tweede Egelantiersdwarsstraat into the heart of the bohemian Jordaan district, very much a local suburb with some unusual shops.

5 Walk on to Lijnbaansgracht, and then turn right on to Lindengracht, once a canal.

Shopping

ANTIEKCENTRUM AMSTERDAM

antiekcentrumamsterdam.nl

A permanent, covered art and antiques market that's the largest in the country. Browse through paintings, silverware, pottery, furniture and curios.

🔲 D5 ✉ Elandsgracht 109 ☎ 624 9038
🚊 Tram 7, 10, 17

AZARIUS

This is just one of several smart shops that specialize in magic mushrooms. Staff are available for advice and tips.

🔲 E6 ✉ Kerkstraat 119 ☎ 626 6907
🚊 Tram 1, 2, 5

BLGK EDELSMEDEN

blgk.nl

The showcase for a group of local jewellery designers, each one of whom takes a different contemporary approach to style. All of them make distinctive pieces at moderate prices.

🔲 E4 ✉ Hartenstraat 28 ☎ 624 8154
🚊 Tram 13, 14, 17

FROZEN FOUNTAIN

frozenfountain.nl

Not only is this striking interiors shop a showcase for up-and-coming Dutch designers, it is a great place to find unusual gifts, ceramics and accessories.

🔲 E5 ✉ Prinsengracht 645 ☎ 622 9375
🚊 Tram 1, 2, 5

GALLERIA D'ARTE RINASCIMENTO

delft-art-gallery.com

Visit this shop for all kinds and quality of Delftware, from the most expensive products of De Koninklijke Porceleyne Fles to cheap souvenirs. It also sells excellent polychrome Makkumware.

🔲 E4 ✉ Prinsengracht 170 ☎ 622 7509
🚊 Tram 13, 14, 17

HET OUD-HOLLANDSCH SNOEPWINKELTJE

snoepwinkeltje.com

Rows of Dutch liquorice and traditional sweets in glass jars are on display here, perfect for the novice who's never tried the salty (or sweet) stuff.

🔲 D4 ✉ Tweede Egelantiersdwarsstraat 2
☎ 420 7390 🚊 Tram 10, 13, 14, 17

HUTSPOT

hutspot.com

A concept shop at its best, with one-stop shopping that includes ethical clothing and original local art for sale, a barbershop and a good café, all spread over stylishly designed departments.

🔲 D4 ✉ Rozengracht 204–210 ☎ 370 8708
🚊 Tram 10, 13, 14, 17

JORDINO

jordino.nl

Locals and tourists line up at this gourmet sweet shop for house-made chocolates, cakes, marzipan, traditional Italian ice cream and sorbet (served with waffle cones), and freshly imported Parisian macaroons.

🔲 E2 ✉ Haarlemmerdijk 25a ☎ 420 3225
🚊 Tram 1, 2, 5, 13, 17

JORRIT HEINEN

jorritheinen.com

This small art gallery and shop also sells Delftware including kitchenware, vases and tiles.

🔲 E6 ✉ Prinsengracht 440 ☎ 627 8299
🚊 Tram 1, 2, 5, 13, 17

JUFFROUW SPLINTER

juffrouwsplinter.nl

The lovely vintage knick-knacks, toys, furniture and items for the home on sale here are sourced from flea markets in the Netherlands, Belgium and France.

There's a notable collection of antique teapots, cups and saucers.

🔢 E4 ✉ Prinsengracht 230 ☎ 330 5515
🚊 Tram 13, 17

DE KINDERBOEKWINKEL

kinderboekwinkel.nl

A well-established children's bookstore that sells both Dutch and English titles. Look out for Dutch authors Dick Bruna (Nijntje series) and Annie M.G. Schmidt (Jip and Janneke series) for classics.

🔢 D4 ✉ Rozengracht 34 ☎ 622 4761
🚊 Tram 13, 14, 17

KITSCH KITCHEN

kitschkitchen.nl

Ghanaian metal furniture, Indian bead curtains, Mexican tablecloths, Chinese pots and pans—the whole world in one very bright kitchen. There's an amazing variety of goods on sale here, including masses of plastic.

🔢 D4 ✉ Rozengracht 8–12 ☎ 462 0051
🚊 Tram 13, 14, 17

MECHANISCH SPEELGOED

Batteries are not included (they're not needed), in these modern versions of classic toys from a kinder, gentler era of playthings. Find well-made wooden dollhouses, costumes, puppets and metal wind-up toys.

🔢 E3 ✉ Westerstraat 67 ☎ 638 1680
🚊 Tram 3, 10

MINT MINI MALL

mintminimall.nl

Pretty pastel gifts for her, him, kids and the home from the latest European designers. Much of the merchandise is made of natural and sustainable materials.

🔢 E5 ✉ Runstraat 27 ☎ 627 2466
🚊 Tram 1, 2, 5, 7, 10, 13, 14, 17

LA SAVONNERIE

savonnerie.nl

A veritable potpourri of natural, hand-made bath-time products. You can even have your own personal text inscribed on the delicious handmade soaps.

🔢 D5 ✉ Prinsengracht 294 ☎ 428 1139
🚊 Tram 13, 14, 17

SHIRDAK

shirdak.nl

For lovers of eastern textiles, try this interesting shop stocking products from central Asia: slippers, rugs, gifts, all in gorgeous hues. It also sells European felt hats, each one a unique design.

🔢 D4 ✉ Prinsengracht 192 ☎ 626 6800
🚊 Tram 13, 14, 17

SPRMRKT

sprmrkt.nl

Part fashion store, part gallery, this former supermarket space is now filled with luxury clothing, beautiful accessories and an excellent coffee bar.

🔢 D4 ✉ Rozengracht 191–193 ☎ 330 5601
🚊 Tram 13, 14, 17

TENUE DE NÎMES

tenuedenimes.com

This is a well-curated selection of the world's best denim labels. You'll find the right pair of jeans here, guaranteed.

🔢 F3 ✉ Haarlemmerstraat 92–94 ☎ 331 2778 🚊 Tram 1, 2, 5, 13, 17

DE WITTE TANDENWINKEL

dewittetandenwinkel.nl

An unusual shop that focuses solely on oral hygiene. There's a huge range of toothbrushes, from electric to novelty, plus toothpaste, floss and other fun stuff for your pearly whites.

🔢 E5 ✉ Runstraat 5 ☎ 623 3443 🚊 Tram 1, 2, 5, 7, 10

Entertainment and Nightlife

BOOM CHICAGO

boomchicago.nl

Grab a bucket of beer, sit down and enjoy the live comedy show often featuring satirical political themes. Famous American alumni of this comedy club include Seth Meyers, Jason Sudeikis and Jordan Peele.

🔲 D4 ✉ Rozengracht 17 ☎ 217 0400
🚋 Tram 13, 14, 17

BOURBON STREET

bourbonstreet.nl

This intimate and friendly venue is great for live jazz, blues, pop, soul, funk and rock & roll. On Mondays, there's no cover charge and you can join in with the house band. Other nights are free before 11pm.

🔲 E6 ✉ Leidsekruisstraat 6–8 ☎ 623 3440
🚋 Tram 7, 10

CAFÉ PAPENEILAND

papeneiland.nl

One of Amsterdam's oldest brown cafés (circa 1642) retains its old world charm with dark wood paneling, Delft-blue tiles and a central cast iron stove. There are even remnants of a secret 17th-century tunnel that ran under the canal to a hidden Catholic church during the Protestant Reformation.

🔲 E3 ✉ Prinsengracht 2 ☎ 624 1989
🚋 Tram 1, 2, 5, 13, 17

CAFÉ 'T SMALLE

t-smalle.nl

Originally an old distillery and *proeflokaal* (tasting house) dating from 1780, this lovely traditional little pub is a local favourite. Inside it's all wood and *gezellig* (cosy), outside there's a pretty canal-front terrace.

🔲 E4 ✉ Egelantiersgracht 12 ☎ 623 9617
🚋 Tram 13, 14, 17

CAFÉ DE TWEE ZWAANTJES

cafedetweezwaantjes.nl

You'll find this tiny and lively local bar from 1928 next door to the Tulip Museum. It's full of Amsterdammers playing the accordion and belting out Dutch *levenslied* (folk music—literally "life song").

🔲 E4 ✉ Prinsengracht 114 ☎ 625 2729
🚋 Tram 13, 14, 17, 20

JAZZ CAFÉ ALTO

jazz-café-alto.nl

Fabulous live jazz and blues are played at this local favourite every evening in a cosy, casual atmosphere. Expect it to be packed and look out for celebrities who frequent this place.

🔲 E6 ✉ Korte Leidsedwarsstraat 115 ☎ 626 3249 🚋 Tram 7, 10, 16

JIMMY WOO

jimmywoo.com

Celebrities are known to frequent this exclusive R&B club and it often has long lines. Inside, there are two floors—a lounge with red booths upstairs and a downstairs dancefloor.

🔲 D6 ✉ Korte Leidsedwarsstraat 18 ☎ 626 3150 🚋 Tram 1, 2, 5, 7, 10

ANCIENT AND MODERN

Brown cafés, so-called because of their smoke-stained ceilings and walls and dark wooden fittings, are reminiscent of the interiors in Dutch old master paintings. Here you can meet the locals in a setting that's *gezellig* (cosy). In stark contrast, there are a growing number of brasserie-like grand cafés and chic, modern bars with stylish, spacious interiors. Watch also for the tiny ancient *proeflokalen* tasting bars (originally distillers' private sampling rooms), serving a host of gins and liqueurs.

Where to Eat

PRICES

Prices are approximate, based on a
3-course meal for one person.

€€€   over €50
€€   €25–€50
€   under €25

BATON BRASSERIE (€)

brasseriebaton.nl

A good choice for a light breakfast or
lunch that's easy on your wallet, this
busy place serves salads, sandwiches
and more, inside on two floors and on a
canalside terrace.

➕ E4 ✉ Herengracht 82, Grachtengordel
☎ 624 8195 ⏰ Mon–Fri 8–6, Sat–Sun 9–6
🚋 Tram 1, 2, 5, 13, 17

DE BELHAMEL (€€€)

belhamel.nl

Art-nouveau style and classical music
set the tone for polished French cuisine
in an intimate, often crowded setting
with a superb canal view.

➕ E3 ✉ Brouwersgracht 60, Grachtengordel
☎ 622 1095 ⏰ Daily 12–4, 6–10 🚋 Tram
1, 2, 5, 13, 17

DE BLAUWE HOLLANDER (€)

deblauwehollander.nl

If it's wholesome Dutch fare at reasona-
ble prices that you're after, The Blue
Dutchman will satisfy. The large portions
may also account for all the tourists.

➕ E6 ✉ Leidsekruisstraat 28, Leidseplein
☎ 627 0521 ⏰ Daily noon–11 🚋 Tram 1,
2, 5, 7, 10

DE BOLHOED (€€)

A colourful and eclectic vegetarian and
vegan restaurant that offers sandwiches,
soups, salads and desserts. The canalside garden patio is a lovely spot for
fine weather days.

➕ E3 ✉ Prinsengracht 60–62, Jordaan
☎ 626 1803 ⏰ Daily 11am–12am 🚋 Tram
13, 14, 17

CAFÉ DUENDE (€€)

café-duende.nl

This Spanish tapas bar is open late, with
food served until 11pm. There are daily
specials and a chef's plate if you want a
blow-out. There's also a flamenco show
on the first Saturday of each month.

➕ E3 ✉ Lindengracht 62, Jordaan ☎ 420
6692 ⏰ Daily 4pm–12am (kitchen 5pm–
11pm) 🚋 Tram 3, 10

MOEDERS (€)

moeders.com

Surrounded by photos of mothers from
all over the world (bring one of your
own to add), Dutch favourites are
dished up with a smile.

➕ D5 ✉ Rozengracht 251, Jordaan ☎ 626
7957 ⏰ Mon–Fri 5pm–2am, Sat–Sun noon–
12am, kitchen closes at 10.30 🚋 Tram 10

LA PERLA (€)

pizzaperla.nl

Italian ingredients imported weekly are
what make the wood-fired thin-crust
pizza at this friendly spot the best in the
city. No reservations? Then get take-out
from their counter across the street.

➕ D4 ✉ Tweede Tuindwarsstraat 14 &
53, Jordaan ☎ 624 8828 ⏰ Daily 10–10
🚋 Tram 10, 13, 14, 17

DUTCH TREATS

Look out for the special Neerlands Dis sign
(a red, white and blue soup tureen), which
indicates restaurants commended for their
quality, traditional Dutch cuisine. A modern
trend is New Dutch cuisine where traditional dishes are prepared with a lighter touch
and a mix of herbs and spices.

PESCA (€€)

pesca-amsterdam.nl

Participate in preparing your own dinner by choosing fresh seafood from a market-like display, then pick the side dishes and drinks. Helpful advice is offered throughout this unique and fun process.

🔲 D4 ✉ Rozengracht 133, Jordaan ☎ 334 5136 🕓 Tue–Thu, Sun 6pm–12am, Fri–Sat 6pm–1am 🚋 Tram 13, 14, 17

PIQNIQ (€)

lunchcafepiqniq.nl

Choose from really good, fresh sandwiches, soups, salads and other items for breakfast or lunch, and enjoy it inside this charming café or eat outside in this picturesque part of the city.

🔲 E3 ✉ Lindengracht 59, Jordaan ☎ 320 3669 🕓 Daily 9–5.30 🚋 Tram 3

POMPADOUR (€)

pompadour.amsterdam

The finest chocolatier in town doubles as a sumptuous tea room. The tiny Louis XVI–style *salon de thé* is the perfect setting to eat the incredibly rich chocolate cakes.

🔲 E5 ✉ Huidenstraat 12, Grachtengordel ☎ 623 9554 🕓 Mon–Fri 10–6, Sat 9–6, Sun 12–6 🚋 Tram 1, 2, 5

SEMHAR (€–€€)

semhar.nl

A wonderful example of Amsterdam's cultural diversity, this Ethiopian/Eritrean place has lots of vegetarian options, and the chicken stew is fantastic.

🔲 D4 ✉ Marnixstraat 259–261, Jordaan ☎ 638 1634 🕓 Tue–Sun 4–10 🚋 Tram 10

TOSCANINI (€€)

restauranttoscanini.nl

This bright, open space is full of locals who have adored this Italian restaurant for years. The organic, made-from-scratch classic dishes never disappoint. Reservations are recommended.

🔲 E3 ✉ Lindengracht 75, Jordaan ☎ 623 2813 🕓 Mon–Sat 6pm–10.30pm 🚋 Tram 3

VAN PUFFELEN (€€)

restaurantvanpuffelen.com

A classic brown café that's also a good restaurant, too. Wholesome French, Italian and Dutch cooking is served in the panelled dining room. Try the local Brouwerij 't IJ beer with an order of *bitterballen*.

🔲 E5 ✉ Prinsengracht 375–377, Grachtengordel ☎ 624 6270 🕓 Mon–Thu 4pm–late, Fri–Sun noon–late 🚋 Tram 13, 14, 17, 20

VINKELES (€€€)

vinkeles.com

Set inside a former 18th century bakery, this ultra-chic Michelin-starred restaurant of The Dylan hotel (▷ 112) serves contemporary French cuisine with an international and fusion twist.

🔲 E5 ✉ Keizersgracht 384, Grachtengordel ☎ 530 2010 🕓 Tue–Sat 7pm–10pm 🚋 Tram 1, 2, 5

WINKEL 43 (€)

winkel43.nl

With a great corner spot by the Noorderkerk, this café is famous for its apple pie. The menu also has typical Dutch fare including *krokets*, *bitterballen* (round versions of the kroket), *uitsmijters* (open sandwich topped with a fried egg) and *stamppot* (potatoes mashed with one or several other vegetables).

🔲 E3 ✉ Noordermarkt 43, Jordaan ☎ 623 0223 🕓 Mon 7am–1am, Tue–Thu 8am–1am, Fri 8am–3am, Sat 7am–3am, Sun 10am–1am 🚋 Tram 10, 13, 14, 17

This is the heart of Amsterdam with its medieval buildings, canals, main shopping streets and the brashness of the Red Light District.

2

3

4

5

6

PRINS

W Ind
Huis

Blm Burg
Wrngerstr
Blm Burg
Vsser Str

Nieuwen

Herengracht

Roomolen
str

Langestr

Singel 7

Singel

Nieuwen

KLUIA

Herenstraat

Blauw.
burgwal

Herengracht

Herengracht

Herengracht
Berg.
str

Singel

SPUISTRAAT

VOORBURGWAL

Nwe Nieuwstr

Nieuwendijk

DAMRAK

Singel

Torenstr

Molst

St Nicolaasstr

Beurs van
Berlage

Beurs-
straat

Beurs-
plein

Warmoesstr

Singel

Singel

**Nieuwe
Kerk**

MOSES EN AARONSTR

CENTRUM

Herengracht

Herengracht

Singel

Singel

Spui-
str

Paleisstraat

**Koninklijk
Paleis**

straat

Dam

**National
Monument**

**Rosse
Buurt**

PALEISSTRAAT

**Madame
Tussauds**

Damstraat

Oudezijds

**Oudezijds
Voorburgwal**

Wilde-
steeg

Kalverstraat

ROKIN

Nes

Nes

Oudezijds

Oude
Doelenstr

Oudezijds

Postzegelmarkt

NIEUWEZIJDS

Spuistraat

Oude
Spiegel-
str

**Amsterdam
Museum**

Oudezijds

Athenaeum
Illustre

Singel

Begijnhof

Het
Lieverdje

**The Amsterdam
Dungeon**

Slijks

**Bijbels
Museum**

Spui

Singel

Voetboog
str

Handboog
str

Kalverstraat

Oudemanhuispoort

Museum

Universiteit

Theater
school

Oude Turfmarkt

**Het
Grachtenhuis**

Beulīng
str

**Franciscus
Xaveriuskerk**

Heiligeweg

Munttoren

Theater

Nwe Doelenstr

Amstel

Koningsplein

Bloemenmarkt

Singel

Munt-
plein

AMSTEL

Herengracht

Reguliersdwarsstraat

Singel

Herengracht

Rijks
inst

| 0 | | 250 m |
| 0 | | 250 yds |

D

E

F

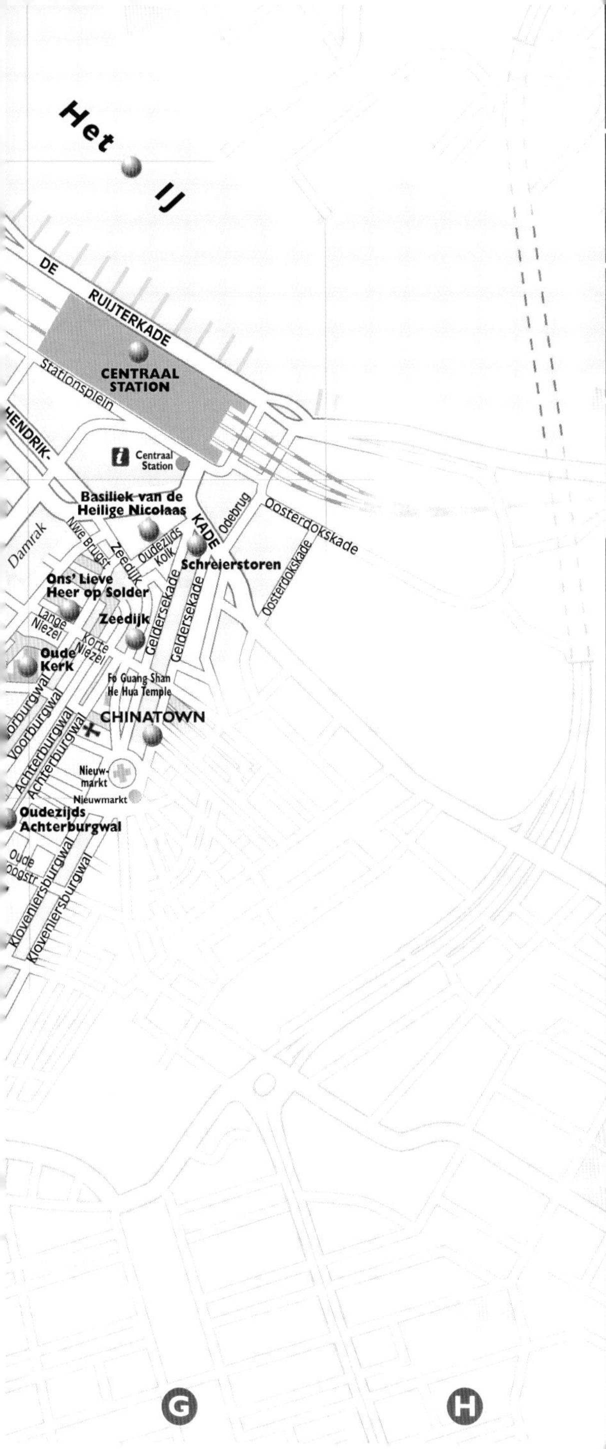

Het IJ

DE RUIJTERKADE

stationsplein

CENTRAAL STATION

HENDRIK-

ℹ️ Centraal Station

Basiliek van de Heilige Nicolaas

Damrak

Nwe Brugst.

Zeedijk

Oudezijds Kolk

KADE

Odebrug

Oosterdokskade

Schreierstoren

Ons' Lieve Heer op Solder

Lange Niezel

Korte Niezel

Gelderskade

Gelderskade

Oosterdokskade

Zeedijk

Oude Kerk

Fo Guang Shan He Hua Temple

Voorburgwal

Oorburgwal

CHINATOWN

Achterburgwal

Achterburgwal

Nieuw-markt

Nieuwmarkt

Oudezijds Achterburgwal

Oude Hoogstr.

Kloveniersburgwal

Kloveniersburgwal

Central Amsterdam

🅖 🅗

Amsterdam Museum

HIGHLIGHTS

● *Bird's eye view of Amsterdam*, Cornelis Anthonisz (1538), the oldest city map
● *The First Steamship on the IJ*, Nicolaas Baur (1816)
● *Girls from the Civic Orphanage*, Nicolaas van der Waay (1880)

TIP

● Make sure you get a plan of the museum as it can be easy to get lost without one.

Try to make this lively and informative museum your first port of call, as once you have a grasp of the city's rich history, your visit will be all the more rewarding.

The building This excellent museum traces the growth of Amsterdam from 13th-century fishing village to bustling metropolis, through an impressive collection of paintings, models, maps and historical objects. They are displayed in one of the city's oldest buildings. Originally a monastery, it was the city orphanage for nearly 400 years, until 1975, when it was converted into a museum. Most of the present structure dates from the 16th and 17th centuries. You can still see evidence of its former use—most notably the ceiling paintings in the Regents' Room and the numerous portraits of children.

Clockwise from left: Detail from a plaque in the Amsterdam Museum; the former Burgerweeshuis (or orphanage) is now the entrance to the museum; 19th-century pharmacy sign; Market Scene by P. Pietersz, 1610; suits of armour on display

The collections The first rooms of the museum chronicle the city's early history and its rise to prominence in trade and commerce. The displays include furniture, memorabilia and a map that illuminates each 25-year period of growth through the centuries. The city's 17th-century Golden Age is covered in detail. Paintings and photographs illustrate the growing welfare problems of the 19th and early 20th centuries, and a small collection of relics from World War II shows how the Nazi occupation affected the population, 10 per cent of which was Jewish.

More art The Amsterdam Gallery (a covered street leading to the museum and free to visit) has original portraits ranging from 1530 to the present day. There's also a 350-year-old wooden Goliath statue to gaze up to.

THE BASICS

amsterdammuseum.nl

✚ F5

✉ Kalverstraat 92, Sint-Luciënsteeg 27

☎ 523 1822

🕐 Daily 10–5

🍴 Mokum Museum Café

🚊 Tram 1, 2, 4, 5, 9, 14, 16

♿ Good

💰 Expensive

❓ Guided tours (1 hour) on request: call in advance

Begijnhof

The preserved buildings of the Begijnhof provided a sanctuary of peace

THE BASICS

nicolaas-parochie.nl
+ E5
⊠ Begijnhof 30, entrance on Spui
🕐 Daily 9–5, enter chapel after 5pm via gate in Spui
🚊 Tram 1, 2, 5
♿ Good
🎫 Free
🛍 Shop

DID YOU KNOW?

● The last Begijn died in 1971.
● The Pilgrim Fathers are said to have worshipped here before leaving for England on the *Speedwell*, prior to crossing the Atlantic in the *Mayflower*.
● Today, the Begijhof is a residence for single women on low incomes, and it has a long waiting list.

Tranquillity characterizes the city's many *hofjes* (almshouses), none more so than this leafy oasis. The cobbled courtyard looks like a film set.

Pious women A tiny gateway leads to the Begijnhof, the oldest and finest *hofje* in the country (almshouses were charitable lodgings for the poor). This secluded community of magnificently restored old houses and gardens around a small church lies a stone's throw from the main shopping thoroughfare. It was built in 1346 as a sanctuary for the Begijnen or Beguines, unmarried women who wanted to live in a religious community without becoming nuns. In return for modest lodging, they devoted themselves to the poor and sick.

Two churches The Begijnenkerk (1419), dominating the courtyard, was confiscated from the Beguines during the Protestant Alteration in 1578. The women continued to worship secretly until religious tolerance was restored in 1795. Meanwhile, their precious church became a warehouse until 1607, when it was given to the city's Scottish Presbyterian community and renamed (or misnamed) the Engelse Kerk (English Church). The simple interior has pulpit panels by Piet Mondrian. Nearby, Het Houten Huys (The Wooden House, 1425) is one of only two remaining wood-fronted houses in Amsterdam. It was built before 1521, when the use of wood as a building material was banned, after a series of fires.

Not just tulips in Amsterdam, the Bloemenmarkt has all kinds of plants on offer

Bloemenmarkt

Golden sunflowers, deep blue irises, delicately scented roses and row upon row of tulips and tulip bulbs create a vibrant display on the market stalls.

Floating market During the 17th and 18th centuries there were approximately 20 floating markets in Amsterdam, at least two of which gratified the Dutch passion for tulips. Nurserymen would sail up the Amstel from their smallholdings and moor here to sell their wares directly from their boats. Today, the stalls at this, the city's only remaining floating market, are permanently moored—and not all of the sales space is actually afloat. Offering a vast variety of seasonal flowers and plants, they are supplied by the florists of Aalsmeer and the region around Haarlem, at the horticultural heart of Holland. More than 16,000 hectares (39,540 acres) are devoted to bulb growing.

Tulip mania Tulips were first spotted in Turkey by Dutch diplomats, who brought them back to Holland around 1600. Shortly after, a Leiden botanist discovered ways of changing their shape and hue, and tulip cultivation rapidly became a national obsession. Prices soared, with single bulbs fetching up to €1,360 (an average worker's annual salary was €68), and an abundance of still life paintings was produced to capture prize blooms on canvas. In 1637, the bubble burst, and many people lost entire fortunes. Prices are more realistic today and tulip bulbs are popular souvenirs.

THE BASICS

⊞ F6

⊠ Singel, between Muntplein and Koningsplein

🕐 Mon–Sat 9–5.30, Sun 11.30–5.30

🚇 Muntplein

🚊 Tram 1, 2, 4, 5, 9, 14, 16

♿ Good

HIGHLIGHTS

● The all-round sensory experience
● The best variety of tulips in the city as well as other types of plants and bulbs
● Decorative wooden tulips

Herengracht

TOP 25

Houses of all shapes and sizes, and with intricate gables, line the banks of Herengracht

THE BASICS

➕ E4

🍴 Bars, cafés, restaurants

🚃 Tram 1, 2, 4, 5, 13, 14, 16, 17

🚌 Hop On-Hop Off stop 3, 6

HIGHLIGHTS

● No. 43–45: Oldest warehouses (1600)
● No. 170–172: Bartolotti Huis
● No. 366: Bijbels Museum (▷ 51)
● No. 409–411: "Twin brothers" facing the "twin sisters" (No. 390–392)
● No. 475: "Jewel of Canal Houses"
● No. 497: Katten Kabinet (Cat Museum)
● No. 502: Huis met de Kolommen (Mayor's residence)
● No. 605: Museum Willet-Holthuysen (▷ 71)

DID YOU KNOW?

● If you stand on the bridge at the junction of Herengracht and Reguliersgracht, you can see 15 bridges simultaneously.

Exploring the city's grandest canal is like going back to Amsterdam's Golden Age. These gilded houses display four centuries of Dutch architectural styles.

The Gentlemen's Canal Herengracht takes its name from the rich merchants and traders of Amsterdam's heyday, and was the first of three concentric canals dug early in the 17th century. Attracting the wealthiest merchants, it has the largest, most ostentatious houses, 400 of which are now protected monuments. The houses had to conform to many building standards, and even the colour of the front doors—known as Amsterdam green—was regulated. As on all canals, taxes were levied according to the width of the canal frontage, hence the rows of tall, narrow residences.

Gable-spotting Owners expressed themselves in the elaborate decoration of their houses' gables and facades. The most common are the step gable and the spout gable. Amsterdam's first neck gable (No. 168) was built in 1638 by Philips Vingboons, and the bell gable became popular early in the 18th century. Around this time, Louis XIV-style facades were considered the height of fashion and No. 475 is a fine example—named the jewel of canal houses.

The Golden Bend Amsterdam's most ornate mansions were built between Leidsestraat and Vijzelstraat, along the stretch of the canal known as the Golden Bend.

The 17th-century Royal Palace, designed by Jacob van Campen, dominates the Dam

TOP 25

Koninklijk Paleis

The Royal Palace is a stunning reminder of the wealth of Amsterdam in its heyday, with lavish decoration inside and out.

Palatial wonder Designed by architect Jacob van Campen in 1648 during the Golden Age, the building originally started life as the town hall. As one of Europe's grandest town halls, its classical design was a startling departure from the Dutch Renaissance style. The poet Constantijn Huygens called it "the world's Eighth Wonder" as the building stands on 13,659 wooden piles to counter the sand beneath.

The details The facade has an astonishing wealth of decoration, with an elaborate pediment and a huge cupola crowned by a galleon weather vane. In front, Atlas holds the weight of the world on his shoulders and the Titan symbolizes the powerful position Amsterdam had during the Golden Age. Inside, the marble floor in the Citizens' Hall features two mid-18th century world maps indicating Amsterdam's colonial influence. The Tribunal was once the city's main courtroom, and condemned prisoners were taken from here to be publicly hanged on the Dam square.

Today In 1808, the town hall was transformed into a royal palace after Napoleon made his brother Louis King of Holland. Today, the building serves as an occasional residence for King Willem-Alexander, while the square is often a meeting place for locals and tourists.

THE BASICS

paleisamsterdam.nl
🔲 F4
✉ Dam
☎ 522 6161
🕐 Daily 10–5, but check for periods of closure
🚃 Tram 1, 2, 4, 5, 9, 13, 14, 16, 17
♿ Good
💰 Expensive

HIGHLIGHTS

● Views of the Dam
● Tribunal
● Citizens' Hall
● Facade

DID YOU KNOW?

● The state bought the palace in 1936 for 10,000 Dutch guilders (equivalent to €5.2 million).
● It is 80m (265ft) long and 56m (125ft) wide.
● The bell tower is 51m (167ft) high.

Nieuwe Kerk

Overlooking the Dam is Nieuwe Kerk (left); the interior (right)

THE BASICS

nieuwekerk.nl
🔲 F4
✉ Dam
☎ 638 6909
🕐 Usually daily 10–5
🍴 't Nieuwe Kafé
🚊 Tram 1, 2, 4, 5, 6, 9, 13, 14, 16, 17
🚌 Hop On-Hop Off stop 7
♿ Good
💷 Varies with exhibitions, but mainly expensive
❓ Regular organ concerts, mostly on Sun. Shop is open daily 10–6, until 10pm on Thu

HIGHLIGHTS

● Organ, Hans Schonat and Jacob Hagerbeer (1650–73)
● Organ case, Jacob van Campen (1645)
● Pulpit, Albert Vinckenbrinck (1644)
● Tomb of Admiral de Ruyter, Rombout Verhulst (1681)

Considering its turbulent history, it is something of a miracle that Holland's magnificent national church has survived. Hearing its organ is a real treat.

Not so new The New Church actually dates from the 15th century, when Amsterdam was growing at such a rate that the Old Church (Oude Kerk, ▷ 48) was no longer sufficient. Construction started in 1408 but the church was destroyed by fire several times. After the Alteration in 1578 (when Amsterdam officially became Protestant), and a further fire in 1645, the church was rebuilt and reconsecrated in 1648. It has no spire: Following years of debate, the money designated for its construction was spent to complete the nearby Stadhuis (Town Hall), which is now the Koninklijk Paleis (▷ 45). It does have one of the finest of Amsterdam's 42 historic church organs—a Schonat-Hagerbeer organ, dating 1650–73, with 5,005 pipes and a full-voiced sound that easily fills the church's vast interior.

Famous names At the time of the Alteration, Amsterdam's churches were largely stripped of their treasures, and the Nieuwe Kerk was no exception. The altar space has since been occupied by the tomb of Holland's most valiant naval hero, Admiral Michiel de Ruyter. Dutch monarchs have been inaugurated here, from Willem I in 1814 to Willem-Alexander in 2013. It is no longer a place of worship, and now hosts exhibitions and recitals.

Inside the tiny "Our Dear Lord in the Attic"

Ons' Lieve Heer op Solder

This tiny museum is one of the city's most surprising places. It is tucked away in a small, inconspicuous canal house close to the Red Light District.

Best-kept secret In 1578, when the Catholic city council was replaced by a Protestant one, Catholic churches were closed throughout the city. In 1661, while Catholic church services were still forbidden, a wealthy merchant named Jan Hartman built a residence on Oudezijds Voorburgwal, and two adjoining houses in Heintje Hoeckssteeg. He ran a sock shop on the ground floor, lived upstairs, rented out the spare rooms in the buildings behind, and cleverly converted the top two floors of the canal house and the attics of all three buildings into a secret Catholic church. Religious freedom only returned with the French occupation in 1795.

Hidden church This *schuilkerk* was just one of many clandestine churches that sprang up throughout the city, but it is one of only a few that has been completely preserved. It was saved from demolition in 1888 by a group of historians called the Amstelkring (Amstel Circle), who nicknamed the church "Our Dear Lord in the Attic". To find a three-level, galleried church at the top of a series of increasingly steep staircases is quite a surprise. Given that there is seating for 200 people, magnificent statuary, silver chalices, paintings, a collapsible altar and a huge organ, it is hard to believe that the services held here were really secret.

THE BASICS

opsolder.nl
🔲 G4
✉ Oudezijds Voorburgwal 38
☎ 624 6604
🕐 Mon–Sat 10–5, Sun, public hols 1–5
🍴 Museum café
Ⓜ Centraal Station
🚊 Tram 1, 2, 4, 5, 9, 13, 16, 17, 26
🚌 Hop On-Hop Off stop 1, 7
♿ None
💶 Expensive
❓ Occasional classical concerts in winter

HIGHLIGHTS

● Church of "Our Dear Lord in the Attic"
● Altar painting *The Baptism of Christ*, Jacob de Wit (1716)
● Priest's bedroom
● Confessional
● Drawing room
● Kitchen
● Treasures from the Cesspit

Oude Kerk

TOP 25

Dating back to the early 14th century, Oude Kerk is the city's oldest building and church

THE BASICS

oudekerk.nl
- ⊞ F4
- ✉ Oudekerksplein 23
- ☎ 625 8284
- 🕐 Mon–Sat 10–6, Sun 1–5.30
- Ⓜ Nieuwmarkt
- 🚋 Tram 4, 9, 16
- ♿ Good
- 💶 Expensive
- ❓ Frequent organ recitals and carillon concerts

HIGHLIGHTS

- ● Great Organ, Vatermüller
- ● Stained-glass windows, Lambert van Noort (1555)
- ● Carillon, François Hemony (1658)
- ● The tombstone of Rembrandt's first wife, Saskia van Uylenburg, which is still in the church even though poverty drove him to sell her grave plot

Surrounded by cafés, bars and sex shops, the Old Church represents an island of spirituality in the Red Light District.

History Amsterdam's oldest building and church is dedicated to St. Nicholas, the patron saint of seafarers. It was built in 1306 to replace a wooden chapel dating from the late 1200s. Over the centuries, the church escaped the great fires that devastated so much of the city, and the imposing basilica you see today dates largely from the 14th century. Its graceful tower, added between 1565 and 1567, contains one of the finest carillons in Holland. In the 16th century Jan Pieterszoon Sweelinck, Holland's best-known composer, was organist here.

Miracle In the 14th century, the Oude Kerk became one of Europe's pilgrimage sights following a miracle: Communion bread regurgitated by a dying man and thrown on the fire didn't burn, and the man did not die. Catholics still take part in the annual *Stille Omgang*, a silent nocturnal procession, but as the Oude Kerk is now Protestant, it no longer follows the ancient pilgrim route to the church, going instead to the Begijnhof.

Sober interior The stark interior has a triple nave and elaborate vaulting. Three magnificent windows in the Lady Chapel survived the Alteration, as did the fine choir stalls. In the 1960s, some 14th-century paintings were found behind layers of blue paint in the vaults.

You'll see plenty of neon in Amsterdam's infamous Red Light District

The Red Light District, bathed in a lurid red neon glow and full of gaping tourists, is one of the city's biggest attractions.

Sex for sale As early as the 15th century, Amsterdam was infamous as a haunt of prostitutes, and the lure of the Red Light District proves irresistible to many visitors today. Crowds clog the narrow alleyways, sex shops, peep shows and suggestively named bars, while prostitutes beckon from their lighted windows. But there is more to the Red Light District than sex. Other people live here too, and go about their everyday business in what, behind the tawdry facade, is an interesting part of the old city. The city council has cut the number of brothels and coffee shops, replacing them with boutiques and other everyday businesses, in an effort to combat organized crime and people-trafficking.

Drug central The area is frequented by drug dealers, and hosts the majority of Amsterdam's marijuana-selling "smoking" coffee shops. The Hash Marihuana & Hemp Museum on Oudezijds Achterburgwal traces the history of hashish and the cannabis plant.

Precautions Watch your wallet, avoid eye contact with undesirable characters, do not take photographs of prostitutes and avoid poorly lit alleyways. Evening is the liveliest time to visit, but don't wander around alone. Be cautious in quiet areas at night, or avoid them completely.

THE BASICS

➕ F4
✉ Borders roughly denoted by Zeedijk (north), Kloveniersburgwal (east), Damstraat (south) and Warmoesstraat (west)
🍴 Restaurants, bars, cafés
🚇 Centraal Station, Nieuwmarkt
🚌 Tram 4, 9, 14, 16

DID YOU KNOW?

● Possession of drugs is technically illegal but the authorities tolerate possession of up to 5g (0.18oz) of soft drugs (cannabis and hash) for personal use.
● Drug-dealing is not allowed. Smoking coffee shops have to be licensed.
● There are some 600 coffee houses in Holland, of which around 150 are in Amsterdam, and some 30,000 home-growers.
● Brothels were legalized in 2000.

Singel

TOP 25

The tree-lined Singel, once the city's first line of defence, is now a residential area

THE BASICS

🛈 F4

✉ Singel

☎ Poezenboot 625 8794; depoezenboot.nl

🕐 Poezenboot Thu–Sat, Mon–Tue 1–3pm

🍴 Cafés and restaurants

🚋 Tram 1, 2, 5, 13, 14, 17

♿ Poezenboot none

✋ Poezenboot by donation

HIGHLIGHTS

● Poezenboot
● Bloemenmarkt (▷ 43)
● Torensluis prison cell
● Munttoren (▷ 52)
● No. 7: narrowest house facade
● No. 2, 36, 74, 83: unusual facades

At first glance, this canal looks like any other major waterway in the city, but here you will find some of Amsterdam's most unusual and enchanting sights.

Former city belt From its construction in the early 15th century until the late 16th century, the city limits were marked by the Singel (originally *Cingle,* meaning belt), the city's defensive moat. Then, in 1586, the city council decided to build quays along Singel's west bank and to convert the moat into a canal for freight ships. Thus Singel became the first of Amsterdam's concentric canals, and its curved shape established the horseshoe layout of the city. With the coming of the railways, canal transportation became less important and Singel began to acquire a residential character. Many warehouses have been converted into homes. The Nieuwe Haarlemmersluis, a sluice gate at the junction of Singel and Brouwersgracht, is opened nightly to top up the city's canals.

All that floats Perhaps the most unusual house is No. 7. The narrowest house front in the city, it was made no wider than a door to minimize property taxes. Opposite is the Poezenboot, a refuge for stray cats. The Torensluis (Tower Lock, on Singel's widest bridge) was used as a prison in the 17th century. The bridge has a monument to Multatuli (1820–87), one of the Netherlands' greatest writers. The floating flower market, the well-known Bloemenmarkt, is also on Singel.

More to See

THE AMSTERDAM DUNGEON
thedungeons.com
Learn a little bit of local dark history through scary but funny interactive adventures with live actors, special effects and more. Not suitable for young children or the faint-hearted.
🔳 F5 ✉ Rokin 78 ☎ 530 8500 ⏱ Daily 11–6 (Fri–Sat to 9) 🚊 Tram 4, 9, 14, 16 ☯ Very expensive

BASILIEK VAN DE HEILIGE NICOLAAS
nicolaas-parochie.nl
The main Roman Catholic church (1888) is one of many Dutch churches named after the patron saint of sailors.
🔳 G4 ✉ Prins Hendrikkade 73 ☎ 624 8749 ⏱ Tue–Fri 11–4, Sat, Mon 12–3, some Sunday mornings/afternoons (varies) 🚊 Tram 1, 2, 4, 5, 9, 13, 16, 17, 26

BIJBELS MUSEUM
bijbelsmuseum.nl
In two historic buildings that are part of the Cromhouthouses, this museum explores the world through one of the oldest and most read books in the world. You can relax in the lovely garden or have a light snack in the Café Cromhout.
🔳 E5 ✉ Herengracht 366–368 ☎ 624 2436 ⏱ Tue–Sun 11–5 🚊 Tram 1, 2, 5 ☯ Moderate

CENTRAAL STATION
Many visitors get their first glimpse of Amsterdam's architectural wonders at Pierre Cuypers' vast neo-Renaissance station (1889), standing with its back to the IJ inlet.
🔳 G3 ✉ Stationsplein 🚇 Centraal Station

CHINATOWN
ibps.nl
Amsterdam's 7,000-strong Chinese community is based around Nieuwmarkt. Take a look at the striking Fo Guang Shan He Hua Temple in Zeedijk, the largest Buddist temple in Europe.
🔳 G4 ✉ Temple: Zeedijk 106–118 ☎ Temple: 420 2357 ⏱ Temple: Tue–Sat 12–5, Sun 10–5 (also Mon Jun–Sep) 🚇 Nieuwmarkt

Centraal Station

FRANCISCUS XAVERIUSKERK
krijtberg.nl

This splendid neo-Gothic church is often dubbed De Krijtberg (Chalk Hill), because it is built on the site of a former chalk merchant's house.

🔢 E5 ✉ Singel 442–448 ☎ 623 1923 🕐 Services only 🚊 Tram 1, 2, 5

HET GRACHTENHUIS
hetgrachtenhuis.nl

The small Museum of the Canals, inside a 17th-century canal house, takes you on a journey through the last 400 years using interactive exhibits and dioramas, and shows you why the city's canals are so special. There's a good gift shop and neat garden to look out for too.

🔢 E5 ✉ Herengracht 386 ☎ 21 1656 🕐 Tue–Sun 10–5 🚊 Tram 1, 2, 5 ♿ Good 💰 Expensive

HET IJ

Amsterdam is on precariously low-lying ground at the confluence of the IJ (an inlet of the IJsselmeer lake). During the city's 17th-century heyday, most maritime activity centred on the IJ and along Prins Hendrikkade, where the old warehouses were crammed with exotic produce from the East. The industrial docks are now to the west, leaving IJ busy with boats, barges and the free shuttle ferries to Amsterdam-Noord from the Waterplein-West dock behind Centraal Station.

🔢 G3 🚉 Centraal Station

MADAME TUSSAUDS
madametussauds.nl

Have your photo taken with world leaders, movie stars, historical figures and top musicians, all cleverly made out of wax, of course.

🔢 F4 ✉ Dam 20 ☎ 523 0623 🕐 Daily 10–10 🚊 Tram 4, 9, 14, 16 ♿ Good 💰 Very expensive

MUNTTOREN

The Mint Tower was originally part of the 15th-century Regulierspoort, one of the main gates of the medieval city wall. It was temporarily

Dam Square's striking Nationaal Monument

Antiquarian books for sale at Oudemanhuispoort

used to mint coin during the 17th century. The carillon, from 1668, consists of 38 bells that chime every 15 minutes.

🟦 F6 ⊠ Muntplein 🚋 Tram 4, 9, 14, 16

NATIONAAL MONUMENT
The 22m (72ft) World War II Memorial obelisk on the Dam contains soil from the then 12 Dutch provinces and the colonies. Every year on 4 May the King lays a wreath here.

🟦 F4 ⊠ Dam 🚋 Tram 4, 9, 14, 16

OUDEMANHUISPOORT
Antiquarian bookstalls line this 18th-century arcade between Oudezijds Achterburgwal and Kloveniersburgwal.

🟦 F5 ⊠ Oudemanhuispoort 🕐 Mon–Sat 11–4 🚋 Tram 1, 2, 5

OUDEZIJDS ACHTERBURGWAL & OUDEZIJDS VOORBURGWAL
In contrast to most of the city's canals, parts of these two are lined with glaring, neon-lit bars and sex shops. Their southern sections are residential and join up with the university campus.

🟦 F5 🚋 Tram 4, 9, 14, 16

SCHREIERSTOREN
Legend has it that the Weeping Tower was where women waved farewell to their seafaring menfolk. They had reason to weep: Voyages took up to four years and many sailors died. Today, the tower houses Café VOC, named after the Vereenigde Oostindische Compagnie (United East India Company) trading house.

🟦 G4 ⊠ Prins Hendrikkade 94–95 🚉 Centraal Station

ZEEDIJK
Once the sea wall of the early maritime settlement and a haunt of sailors and shady characters, this area on the fringe of the Red Light District is home to Chinatown and a parade of bars and restaurants.

🟦 G4 🚉 Centraal Station 🚋 Tram 1, 2, 4, 5, 9, 13, 16, 17, 26

Detail of Schreierstoren, the Weeping Tower

Markets and Museums

A walk around the central area of the city, taking in some of the cultural venues, plus a chance to see some markets en route.

DISTANCE: 2km (1 mile) **ALLOW:** 1 hour

START

DAM ✛ F4
🚊 Tram 4, 9, 13, 14, 16, 17

① Leaving the Dam via Paleisstraat, turn left on to Nieuwezijds Voorburgwal, where a stamp and coin market, Postzegelmarkt, is held.

② Approximately 100m (100 yards) further on the left, Sint-Luciënsteeg brings you to the excellent and informative Amsterdam Museum (▷ 40–41).

③ Pass through the "museum street" Amsterdam Gallery to Gedempte Begijnensloot. At the southern end, a stone archway on your right brings you into the Begijnhof (▷ 42) courtyard.

④ A further archway leads to Spui. On Friday, stalls sell old books, and on Sundays paintings. Head across the square and turn left along the edge of Singel (▷ 50).

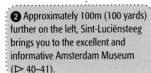

END

DAM ✛ F4
🚊 Tram 4, 9, 13, 14, 16, 17

⑧ Ahead of you is the Nationaal Monument (▷ 53), a striking landmark on the Dam, bringing you back to the start of your walk.

⑦ The museum includes a fine Egyptian collection among its ancient cultural displays. Turn left after the museum over the canal and head first right up busy Rokin, with its antiques shops. At the end, on the left, is Madame Tussauds (▷ 52)

⑥ Your next landmark is the Munttoren (▷ 52) on the left at Muntplein. Cross over the canal (Rokin) and take first left on to Oude Turfmarkt where you will find the Allard Pierson Museum on your right with its collection of antiquities.

⑤ Cross the bridge on to Koningsplein to the popular flower market, the Bloemenmarkt (▷ 43).

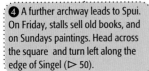

Shopping

AMERICAN BOOK CENTER

abc.nl

Here you'll find four floors of English-language books, as well as US and British magazines and newspapers. Want your own work printed? Their Espresso Book Machine can do that, and they can try to sell it for you too.

➕ F5 ✉ Spui 12 ☎ 625 5537 🚋 Tram 1, 2, 5

AMSTERDAM VINTAGE WATCHES

amsterdamvintagewatches.com

Collectors and connoisseurs alike will appreciate finding classic Cartier, Rolex, Breitling, Patek Philippe and more here. They also stock Mondani books and magazines about wristwatches, which contain information on famous watch brands.

➕ F5 ✉ Singel 414 ☎ 638 0296 🚋 Tram 4, 9, 14, 16

ARCHITECTURA & NATURA

architectura.nl

This shop has been selling new and vintage books on architecture, natural history and landscaping for more than 75 years. Most of the titles are in English and helpful staff are on hand with recommendations.

➕ F3 ✉ Leliegracht 22 ☎ 623 6186 🚋 Tram 13, 14, 17

DE BIERKONING

debierkoning.nl

With more than 2,000 varieties of beer on sale, mostly from Belgium, Germany, the UK and, of course, the Netherlands, this is a proper beer store. Ask the friendly staff for help to select your favourites. They sell all sorts of beer glasses as well.

➕ E5 ✉ Paleisstraat 125 ☎ 625 2336 🚋 Tram 1, 2, 5, 13, 14, 17

DE BIJENKORF

debijenkorf.nl

Founded in Amsterdam in 1870 by Simon Philip Goudsmit, this chain of luxury department stores started off selling haberdashery. The branch at this particular location has been open since 1915 and it has an excellent cafeteria (Kitchen ▷ 62) with great views on the top floor.

➕ F4 ✉ Dam 1 ☎ 0800 0818 🚋 Tram 4, 9, 16

THE BOOK EXCHANGE

bookexchange.nl

Situated across a lovely canal, this second-hand English bookshop has excellent prices. Steep stairs take you up to various floors, all stacked full of books on travel, hobbies, social science, politics, psychology, French and German literature, as well as fiction. The owner is available to answer queries.

➕ F5 ✉ Kloveniersburgwal 58 ☎ 626 6266 🚋 Tram 4, 9, 14, 16

BYAMFI

amfi.nl

For one-of-a-kind pieces, visit this gallery-like clothing store showcasing the latest creations by students, teachers and alumni from the Amsterdam Fashion Institute (AMFI).

➕ F5 ✉ Spui 23 ☎ 525 8133 🚋 Tram 1, 2, 5

CONDOMERIE

condomerie.com

This specialty condom shop (the world's first) makes for an entertaining but also interesting visit. The staff are knowledgeable and the wares come in all shapes, sizes and colours.

➕ F4 ✉ Warmoesstraat 141 ☎ 627 4174 🚋 Tram 4, 9, 14, 16

DAM SQUARE SOUVENIRS

dutchsouvenirs.com

A giant yellow clog alerts tourists to this spacious shop that sells lovely ceramics, t-shirts, magnets, postcards, tulips, umbrellas, and yes, wooden clogs. Lots and lots of them.

➕ F4 ✉ Dam 17 ☎ 620 3432 🚋 Tram 4, 9, 14, 16

DROOG

droog.com

The Dutch love concept shops and this is one of the best in the city. Mingle with the creative crowd in this fantastic art gallery, café, clothing store, furniture store and hotel all-in-one. The lush courtyard is amazing too.

➕ F5 ✉ Staalstraat 7B ☎ 523 5059 🚋 Tram 4, 9, 14

DUN YONG

dunyong.com

Right in the middle of Chinatown, this large department store specializes in Asian goods. Hard-to-find imported groceries, cookware, prepared foods and even furniture are spread across fours floors.

➕ G4 ✉ Stormsteeg 9 ☎ 622 1763 🚋 Tram 4, 9, 16, 26

TIPS

Most shops are open Tuesday to Saturday from 9am or 10am until 6pm, on Monday from 1pm until 6pm, on Thursday until 9pm. Many shops open 12–5pm on Sunday, too. Cash is the normal method of payment, although credit cards are accepted at nearly all department stores and most of the larger shops. If you want to browse in the smaller shops it is customary to greet the owner who will be only too happy for you to look around.

GASTRONOMIE NOSTALGIE

gastronomienostalgie.nl

The tableware on sale here is the type used in the heyday of hotels such as the Ritz, the Carlton and the Hotel de Paris. It specializes in antique silver, silver-plated objects, porcelain, glass and crystal.

➕ E5 ✉ Nieuwezijds Voorburgwal 304 ☎ 422 6226 🚋 Tram 1, 2, 5

THE HEADSHOP

headshop.nl

The shop for marijuana paraphernalia and memorabilia ever since it opened in the 1960s.

➕ G5 ✉ Kloveniersburgwal 39 ☎ 624 9061 🚇 Nieuwmarkt

HEMPSHOPPER

hempshopper.com

Purveyor of snacks, pet food, clothing, accessories and cosmetics that are all made of hemp.

➕ F3 ✉ Singel 10 ☎ 773 7014 🚋 Tram 1, 2, 5, 13, 17

HET HANZEN HUIS

hethanzehuis.nl

Step back in time and find teas, coffees, sweets and other fine items beautifully packaged and made by the original Hanseatic League trading partners.

➕ F5 ✉ Staalstraat 20 ☎ 330 3632 🚋 Tram 4, 9, 14, 16

H.P. DE VRENG & ZONEN

oudamsterdam.nl

Celebrated wine-and-spirits establishment since 1710 and producer of fine liqueurs and *jenevers* (gin) since 1852. Their unusual bottle collection is interesting, and they have a collection of more than 15,000 miniature bottles.

➕ F4 ✉ Nieuwendijk 75 ☎ 624 4581 🚋 Tram 1, 2, 5, 13, 17

JACOB HOOY

jacob-hooy.nl

In 1743, Jacob Hooy opened a spice stall at the Amsterdam Nieuwmarkt. The business has been running ever since and is now in the form of this old-fashioned apothecary, selling herbs, spices and homeopathic remedies. The shop is full of earthenware jars and 19th-century furniture. They sell black liquorice, too.

🟦 G5 ✉ Kloveniersburgwal 10–12 ☎ 624 3041 🚇 Nieuwmarkt

KALVERTOREN

kalvertoren.nl

On rainy days, this modern shopping mall makes for a good escape. It includes popular Dutch discount store HEMA and it has a rooftop café with nice views of the city centre.

🟦 F5 ✉ Kalverstraat 212–220 ☎ 427 3901 🚋 Tram 1, 2, 4, 5, 9, 14, 16

KOKO COFFEE & DESIGN

ilovekoko.com

Dutch and Scandinavian designers showcase their creations alongside delicious sweet and savoury snacks and excellent coffee in a modish space in the Red Light District.

🟦 F5 ✉ Oudezijds Achterburgwal 145 ☎ 626 4208 🚋 Tram 4, 9, 14, 16

LAMBIEK

lambiek.net

Possibly the world's oldest comic dealer, the legendary Lambiek is the place to pick up obscure graphic novels as well as classics such as Suske en Wiske, Kuifje and Donald Duck. There's also a gallery area that sells artwork and look out for the special events, such as workshops and book signings.

🟦 G4 ✉ Koningsstraat 27 ☎ 626 7543 🚇 Nieuwmarkt

MAGNA PLAZA

magnaplaza.nl

Amsterdam's most impressive-looking shopping mall is in an imposing neo-Gothic building that was formerly the city's main post office. The interior is just as stunning. The ground-floor café is perfect for people-watching.

🟦 E4 ✉ Nieuwezijds Voorburgwal 182 ☎ 620 8977 🚋 Tram 1, 2, 5, 13, 14, 17

OQIUM

oqium.nl

This shoe shop is a paradise for lovers of trainers. Its focus is on high tops, especially Air Jordans. Have a look at the display of rare and unusual trainers, most of which belong to the owner.

🟦 E5 ✉ Nieuwezijds Voorburgwal 262 ☎ 262 0922 🚋 Tram 1, 2, 5

P.G.C. HAJENIUS

hajenius.com

One of the world's finest tobacco shops, P.G.C. Hajenius has been selling cigars since 1826. It's housed in an elegant art deco building, with knowledgeable staff and a smoking lounge. It's such a welcoming place that it's worth a visit even for non-smokers.

🟦 F5 ✉ Rokin 92–96 ☎ 623 7494 🚋 Tram 4, 9, 14, 16

SCHELTEMA

scheltema.nl

The first Scheltema opened in 1853 and now it's the city's largest bookstore: you'll find what you are looking for with more than 125,000 titles in Dutch and English, spread over five floors. The used books selection is excellent and there are weekly book-signing events.

➕ F5 ✉ Rokin 9 ☎ 523 1411 🚋 Tram 4, 9, 14, 16

WEBERS HOLLAND

webersholland.nl

Hidden behind the facade of the historic Klein Trippenhuis, one of the city's narrowest houses, former graphic designer Désirée Webers sells sexy PVC cat suits, party wear, fantastical high heels and thigh-high boots.

➕ G5 ✉ Kloveniersburgwal 26 ☎ 638 1777 🚇 Nieuwmarkt

WONDERWOOD

wonderwood.nl

Plywood has never looked more beautiful than at this gallery store of new, re-edition and vintage designer furniture from the 1940s to the 1960s. Admire works by Breuer, Eames and more.

➕ F5 ✉ Rusland 3 ☎ 625 3738 🚋 Tram 4, 9, 14, 16

Entertainment and Nightlife

AKHNATON

akhnaton.nl

Founded in the 1950s by a group of students, this club continues to be popular and has live music and DJs playing reggae, salsa, soul and other world music. Some nights are for dance lessons and others are for the LGBTQ community.

➕ F4 ✉ Nieuwezijds Kolk 25 ☎ 624 3396 🚋 Tram 1, 2, 5, 13, 17

AMSTERDAM MAGIC SHOW

amsterdam-magic.com

Top illusionists, magicians and mind-readers entertain in English at the charming vintage theatre of the Paleis van de Weemoed in the Red Light District. Book tickets early as these shows are only twice a month, for now.

➕ G4 ✉ Oudezijds Voorburgwal 15–17 ☎ 808 5384 🚇 Nieuwmarkt

AMSTERDAMS MARIONETTEN THEATER

marionettentheater.nl

Young and old will enjoy watching this live puppet show. The large, traditional

BAR TALK

Most of the hundreds of bars and cafés in Amsterdam are open from around 10am until the early hours and many serve meals. *Proeflokalen* (tasting houses) open from around 4pm, and some serve snacks, such as nuts, cheese, meatballs and sausage. Beer is the most popular alcoholic drink. It is always served with a head, and often with a chaser called a *kopstoot* (a blow to the head). If you want only a small beer, ask for a *colatje* or *kleintjepils*. Belgian beers are increasingly popular in Holland, and are considered more of a craft product.

wooden marionettes are dressed in period costumes and the performances are of operas, often by Mozart, sung in Dutch.

🔼 G4 ✉ Nieuwe Jonkerstraat 8
☎ 620 8027 🚇 Nieuwmarkt

BEURS VAN BERLAGE

beursvanberlage.nl

Home to the Netherlands Philharmonic Orchestra and the Netherlands Chamber Orchestra, this remarkable early modernist building, which once housed the stock exchange, makes an impressive concert hall, festival and exhibit venue. The café has a nice Dutch menu.

🔼 F4 ✉ Damrak 243 ☎ 530 4141
🚋 Tram 4, 9, 14, 16

CAFÉ HOPPE

caféhoppe.com

One of the most popular brown cafés, Hoppe dates back to 1670, as is evident by the antique casks that line the wall. The prices for drinks are good but be prepared for crowds.

🔼 E5 ✉ Spui 18–20 ☎ 420 4420
🚋 Tram 1, 2, 5

CAFÉ DE JAREN

cafedejaren.nl

A spacious, ultramodern café that's often busy with a mixed crowd of students, locals and tourists. The restaurant on the second level has a good salad buffet. For fine weather, there are sunny terraces overlooking the Amstel.

🔼 F5 ✉ Nieuwe Doelenstraat 20–22
☎ 625 5771 🚋 Tram 4, 9, 14, 16

DE DRIE FLESCHJES

dedriefleschjes.nl

Locals have been sipping *jenever* (Dutch gin) at this tasting house since 1650. Some of the old wooden casks

---

> **DUTCH COURAGE**
>
> Dutch gin, or *jenever*, from malted grains and juniper berries, comes in two distinct categories: *jonge* (young—generally a neutral taste) and *oude* (old—smoother and more aromatic). These terms don't refer to any aging of the spirit, but rather the new or old style of making jenever. Other interesting tastes may be added; try *bessenjenever* (blackcurrant), or *citroenjenever* (lemon). *Jenever* is drunk straight or as a beer chaser, not with a mixer. Dutch for cheers is *Proost!*

on the wall are padlocked and privately owned. The sandy floor adds to the charm of this little place.

🔼 F4 ✉ Gravenstraat 18 ☎ 624 8443
🚋 Tram 1, 2, 4, 5, 9, 13, 14, 16, 17

DE ENGELBEWAARDER

cafe-de-engelbewaarder.nl

Once a literary bar from the 1970s, this arty café has a large selection of beers on tap and a Dutch pub menu to enjoy by the canal. And being a café in Amsterdam, customers can even dock their boats right outside. On Sunday afternoons there's a live jazz band that has a loyal local following.

🔼 F5 ✉ Kloveniersburgwal 59 ☎ 625 3772
🚇 Nieuwmarkt

DE OOIEVAAR

proeflokaaldeooievaar.nl

Upon exiting Centraal Station, you should head straight to one of the smallest and friendliest *proeflokalen* (▷ 58) in the Netherlands. Taste some traditional *jenever* (Dutch gin), eat a hardboiled egg, and have a chat with the barman.

🔼 G4 ✉ Sint Olofspoort 1 ☎ 625 7360
🚋 1, 2, 4, 5, 9, 13, 16, 17, 26

PATHÉ TUSCHINSKI

pathe.nl/bioscoop/tuschinski

An art deco marvel, this cinema was built in 1921 and is one of the world's most beautiful. Pick any movie that's playing in the main hall and book the private balcony package for a real treat.
➕ F6 ✉ Reguliersbreestraat 26–34 ☎ 428 1060 🚋 Tram 4, 9, 14

SUPPERCLUB

supperclub.amsterdam

This is more than just dinner. Eat off your lap while reclining on a bed and take a massage between courses, all listening to music. Anything goes here and it is not for the sensitive or prudish.
➕ F6 ✉ Singel 460 ☎ 344 6400 🚋 Tram 1, 2, 5

WINSTON KINGDOM

winston.nl

Live indie rock, punk, hip hop and electro, with burlesque shows mixed in, is the hallmark of this party-hard dive bar. It's very popular with students and backpackers, particularly as there's a hostel next door with a good breakfast.
➕ F4 ✉ Warmoesstraat 129 ☎ 623 1380 🚋 Tram 4, 9, 14, 16

WYNAND FOCKINK

wynand-fockink.nl

Down a side alley, this 1679 *proeflokaal* serves 100 or so gins and liqueurs. If the weather is warm, seek out the courtyard garden.
➕ F4 ✉ Pijlsteeg 31–43 ☎ 639 2695 🚋 Tram 4, 9, 14, 16

Where to Eat

<table>
<tr><td colspan="2">PRICES</td></tr>
<tr><td colspan="2">Prices are approximate, based on a 3-course meal for one person.</td></tr>
<tr><td>€€€</td><td>over €50</td></tr>
<tr><td>€€</td><td>€25–€50</td></tr>
<tr><td>€</td><td>under €25</td></tr>
</table>

1E KLAS (€€)

restaurant1eklas.nl

This café-restaurant (pronounced "Eerste Klas") is on Platform 2B in the old, 1880s first-class waiting rooms at Amsterdam's Centraal Station. Enjoy French and Dutch cuisine in the grand old style of steam travel. The adjacent pub is a relaxing spot for a beer while waiting for your train.
➕ G3 ✉ Centraal Station, Stationsplein 15, Centrum ☎ 625 0131 🕐 Daily 8.30am–11pm 🚋 Tram 1, 2, 4, 5, 9, 13, 16, 17, 26

ANEKA RASA (€€)

anekarasa.nl

A great place to try authentic and refreshingly inexpensive Indonesian *rijsttafel*. Portions are generous and the service is good.
➕ G4 ✉ Warmoesstraat 25–29, Centrum ☎ 626 1560 🕐 Daily 5–10 🚋 Tram 4, 9, 16, 26

BORD'EAU (€€€)

bordeau.nl

The Michelin-starred restaurant of the De l'Europe hotel, overlooking the River

Amstel, has top-flight French cuisine, an impressive wine list as well as plush good looks.

🔲 F5 ✉ Nieuwe Doelenstraat 2–8, Centrum ☎ 531 1705 🕐 Tue–Fri 12–2.30, 6.30–10.30, Sat 6.30–10.30 🚊 Tram 4, 9, 14, 16

BRIDGES (€€€)

bridgesrestaurant.nl

Along the oldest canal in the city, on the site of the former City Hall, this Michelin-starred restaurant serves fish with inventive French flair. The modernist dining area features an original Karel Appel mural, and the courtyard area is beautiful.

🔲 F4 ✉ The Grand hotel, Oudezijds Voorburgwal 197, Centrum ☎ 555 3560 🕐 Tue–Fri 12–2.30, 6.30–10.30, Sat–Sun 1–3, 6.30–10.30 🚇 Nieuwmarkt 🚊 Tram 4, 9, 14, 16

CAFÉ BERN (€€)

cafebern.com

Open since 1978, the Swiss menu here hasn't changed a bit, nor does it need to. The cheese fondue and the entrecôte (that you cook yourself) are their bestsellers. Service is welcoming and relaxed.

🔲 G4 ✉ Nieuwmarkt 9, Centrum ☎ 622 0034 🕐 Daily 4pm–1am (kitchen 6pm–11pm) 🚇 Nieuwmarkt

CAFÉ LUXEMBOURG (€–€€)

luxembourg.nl

Watch the world go by over a slice of cheesecake or a club sandwich on the terrace of this grand café. Their reading table is stocked with international newspapers and magazines (a common sight in Dutch cafés).

🔲 E5 ✉ Spui 24, Centrum ✉ 620 6264 🕐 Mon–Fri 8am–late, Sat–Sun 9am–late 🚊 Tram 1, 2, 5

CHEZ GEORGES (€€€)

chez-georges.nl

Chez Georges serves classic French cuisine in its stylish restaurant, which stretches over three floors. There's an inventive daily five-course tasting menu made fresh from whatever's in the market that morning.

🔲 E4 ✉ Herenstraat 3, Grachtengordel ☎ 626 3332 🕐 Tue–Sun 6–11pm 🚊 Tram 1, 2, 5, 13, 14, 17

GARTINE (€)

gartine.nl

Many of the ingredients used at this laid-back but busy little brunch spot are sourced from the owner's own garden and orchard. Prices are great and they offer a wonderful afternoon tea here as well. Reservations are recommended.

🔲 F5 ✉ Taksteeg 7, Centrum ☎ 320 4132 🕐 Wed–Sat 10–6 🚊 Tram 1, 2, 4, 5, 9, 14, 16

GEISHA (€€)

restaurantgeisha.nl

Try Chinese, Japanese, Thai and Korean dishes all in one night at this dimly lit modern Asian restaurant. Afterwards, head over to Porem, the sleek cocktail bar below.

🔲 G4 ✉ Prins Hendrikkade 106, Centrum
☎ 626 2410 🕐 Mon–Sat 6–11 🚋 Tram 4,
9, 16, 26

GREENWOOD'S (€)

greenwoods.eu

This little English-style tearoom serves
wonderful all day breakfasts, lunch and
traditional cream teas. They offer a picnic
service as well, perfect for on the boat or
at the park.

🔲 F4 ✉ Singel 103, Grachtengordel ☎ 623
7071 🕐 Mon–Thu 9.30–6, Fri–Sun 9.30–7
🚋 Tram 1, 2, 5, 13, 17

HAESJE CLAES (€€)

haesjeclaes.nl

Classic Dutch comfort food is served
in this maze of seven wood-panelled
dining rooms in a building dating from
the 16th century. The walls are adorned
with interesting tiles, paintings, maps,
mirrors and photos.

🔲 E5 ✉ Spuistraat 273–275, Centrum
☎ 624 9998 🕐 Daily noon–10 🚋 Tram
1, 2, 5

IN DE WAAG (€€)

indewaag.nl

Inside a medieval 15th-century
former city gate and later, a weigh
house and museum, this restaurant-café
is lit by hundreds of candles, adding to
the richly historic atmosphere. Dutch
favourites are on the menu.

🔲 G4 ✉ Nieuwmarkt 4, Centrum ☎ 422
7772 🕐 Thu–Sun 9am–late, Mon–Wed 11am–
late (dinner until 10.30pm) 🚇 Nieuwmarkt

KANTJIL & DE TIGER (€€)

kantjil.nl

This modern, good-value Indonesian
restaurant serves delicious *rijsttafel* in a
central location that gets lively in the
evening. It's family-friendly with high

chairs available, and try their refreshing
home-made iced tea. The Kantjil To Go
next door offers quick take-out.

🔲 E5 ✉ Spuistraat 291–293, Centrum
☎ 620 0994 🕐 Daily noon–11pm 🚋 Tram
1, 2, 5

KITCHEN (€)

debijenkorf.nl

On the top floor of De Bijenkorf department store (▷ 55), with views of the
Dam, this upmarket cafeteria is good
value for money. Choose from fresh
juices, salads, noodles, pizza, steak,
sushi, sandwiches, ice cream, cakes and
more besides.

🔲 F4 ✉ Dam 1, Centrum ☎ 552 1772
🕐 Daily 10–8 🚋 Tram 4, 9, 14, 16

KWEKKEBOOM (€)

kwekkeboom.nl

Famous for its *krokets*, this patisserie
has been in business since 1890.
The pastries are delicious too, especially
the *tompouce* (a bit like a vanilla slice).
For New Year's Eve only, they sell a truly
traditional Dutch treat—*oliebollen*
(similar to a donut but better).

🔲 F6 ✉ Reguliersbreestraat 36 ☎ 623 1205
🕐 Mon–Sat 9–5.45, Sun noon–6 🚋 Tram
4, 9, 14

LATEI (€)

latei.net

This funky eatery and thrift shop all-in-one has a simple, mostly organic, vegetarian snack menu. The coffee's very good too. Like what you see on the wall? It's for sale, as is almost everything else inside.

🔼 G4 ✉ Zeedijk 143, Centrum ☎ 625 7485 🕐 Mon–Wed 8am–6pm, Thu–Fri 8am–10pm, Sat 9am–10pm, Sun 10am–6pm 🚇 Nieuwmarkt 🚋 Tram 4, 9, 14, 16

MAXIMILIAAN (€€)

maximiliaan-amsterdam.com

Since 1870, this popular brasserie on the site of a former 16th-century brewery, has sold nearly 6 million "numbered" steaks. If a lucky diner gets a number ending in 00, they receive a free bottle of house wine.

🔼 F4 ✉ Hotel Die Port van Cleve, Nieuwezijds Voorburgwal 176, Centrum ☎ 714 2000 🕐 Daily 7am–10.30am, 12–5pm, 6pm–10pm 🚋 Tram 1, 2, 5, 13, 17

MORITA-YA (€€)

This Japanese-owned, little sushi spot has been a local favourite for years. Nothing fancy, just consistently good, fresh sushi and sashimi.

🔼 G4 ✉ Zeedijk 18, Centrum ☎ 638 0756 🕐 Tue–Sun 6pm–10pm 🚋 Tram 1, 2, 4, 5, 9, 13, 16, 17, 26

NORLING RESTAURANT (€€)

norling.nl

Tibetan owner and chef Tenzing prepares slow-cooked, rich stews and curries with authentic Himalayan flavours and spices. A comforting meal in equally comforting surroundings.

🔼 E6 ✉ Reguliersdwarsstraat 23, Centrum ☎ 434 5433 🕐 Daily 5pm–11pm 🚋 Tram 1, 2, 5

PANNENKOEKENHUIS UPSTAIRS (€)

upstairspannenkoeken.nl

Inside a 16th-century home, up a set of steep steps, you'll find this tiny restaurant serving some of the best sweet and savory Dutch pancakes in town. With more than 100 teapots hanging from the ceiling but only a few tables available, reservations are a must.

🔼 F5 ✉ Grimburgwal 2 ☎ 626 5603 🕐 Wed–Sat noon–6pm, Sun noon–5pm 🚋 Tram 4, 9, 14, 16

ROSE'S CANTINA (€€)

rosescantina.com

A lively, atmospheric Mexican restaurant and bar that gets loud and crowded. The cocktails are very good and the food is rich and flavourful. During the warmer months they open up the lovely garden terrace.

🔼 F6 ✉ Reguliersdwarsstraat 38–40, Centrum ☎ 625 9797 🕐 Sun–Thu 5pm–1am, Fri–Sat 5pm–3am 🚋 Tram 4, 9, 14, 16

DE SILVEREN SPIEGEL (€€€)

desilverenspiegel.com

A short but exquisite classic menu, complemented by one of the city's best wine lists, is on offer in a superbly

restored 1614 house. There's a terrace for dining alfresco in fine weather.

⊞ F3 ⊠ Kattengat 4–6, Centrum ☎ 624 6589 ⏰ Mon–Sat 6–10 🚋 Tram 1, 2, 5, 13, 17

THAISE SNACKBAR BIRD (€)

thaibird.nl

This is one of the better take-outs on Chinatown's Zeedijk, and its spring rolls and spare ribs make for a delicious snack. There's a sit-down version across the street but it's a tad more expensive.

⊞ G4 ⊠ Zeedijk 77, Centrum ☎ 420 6289 ⏰ Mon–Wed 1pm–10pm, Thu–Sun 1pm–10.30pm 🚋 Tram 4, 9, 16 Ⓜ Nieuwmarkt

TOASTABLE (€)

toastable.nl

On offer here are triple-decker grilled cheese sandwiches that are sure to satisfy, plus create-your-own breakfasts, good coffee, and freshly squeezed juices. Located just across the canal from the Bloemenmarkt.

⊞ F6 ⊠ Singel 441, Centrum ⊠ 626 2969 ⏰ Daily 8–5 🚋 Tram 1, 2, 5

TOMAZ (€€)

tomaz.nl

This friendly restaurant consists of two beautifully restored 17th-century buildings and features an upstairs terrace with a view. The food is traditional home-made Dutch with a modern twist. There's a selection of board games that you can play, too.

⊞ F5 ⊠ Begijnensteeg 6–8, Centrum ☎ 320 6489 ⏰ Daily noon–10pm 🚋 Tram 1, 2, 4, 5, 9, 14, 16, 24, 25

VAN KERKWIJK (€€)

caferestaurantvankerkwijk.nl

Tucked away on a quiet street, just steps from busy Dam Square, this modest and friendly café has no printed menu and the varied selection of superb dishes changes daily. You'll probably have to wait at this hot spot, so grab a seat at the bar.

⊞ F5 ⊠ Nes 41, Centrum ☎ 620 3316 ⏰ Daily 11am–late 🚋 Tram 4, 9, 14, 16

D'VIJFF VLIEGHEN (€€–€€€)

vijffvlieghen.nl

The menu in the Five Flies—five 17th-century houses—has an impressive collection of New Dutch dishes, which are imaginative and beautifully presented. The set meal is good value. You might find yourself sitting next to a Rembrandt etching.

⊞ F5 ⊠ Spuistraat 294–302, Centrum ☎ 530 4060 ⏰ Daily 6–10 🚋 Tram 1, 2, 5

WOK TO WALK (€)

woktowalk.com

This branch of a Thai chain is well worth knowing about if you need a late-night meal in central Amsterdam. Choose your ingredients and see them cooked freshly for you. Especially good for vegetarians.

⊞ F4 ⊠ Warmoesstraat 85 ☎ 427 6960 ⏰ Sun–Thu 11am–3am, Fri–Sat 11am–4am 🚋 Tram 4, 9, 14, 16

COFFEE SHOPS

In Amsterdam, the expression coffee shop refers to the "smoking" coffee shops, where people hang out, high on hash. Smoking coffee shops are usually easily recognizable by their psychedelic decor, thick fog of bitter smoke and mellow clientele. The cake on sale is sure to be drug-laced "space cake." Surprisingly, many such shops do a good cup of coffee. For just coffee, you need to look out for a straightforward café or *koffiehuis*, or coffee bar.

The district lying to the east of the hub of the city has a different feel. Here you are away from the tourists, with residential housing and modern development set within the canals and docks.

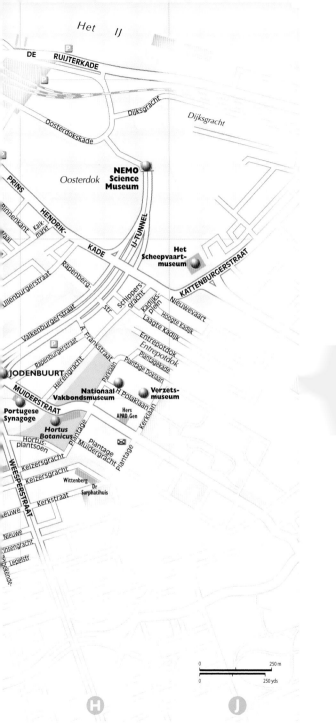

Het IJ

DE RUIJTERKADE

Dijksgracht

Dijksgracht

Oosterdokskade

PRINS

Oosterdok

NEMO Science Museum

Binnenkant

HENDRIK-

Kalk-markt

KADE

IJ-TUNNEL

Het Scheepvaart-museum

KATTENBURGERSTRAAT

Rapenberg

str

Schippersgracht

Kadijks plein

Nieuwevaart

Hoogte Kadijk

Valkenburgerstraat

Laagte Kadijk

A Frankstraat

Entrepotdok

Rapenburgerstraat

Entrepotdok

Plantagekade

Herengracht

JODENBUURT

Parklaan

Plantage Doklaan

Nationaal Vakbondsmuseum

Polaklaan

Verzets-museum

MUIDERSTRAAT

Portugese Synagoge

Hers APAD Gen

Kerklaan

Hortus Botanicus

Plantage

Hortus-plantsoen

Plantage Muidergracht

Plantage

Keizersgracht

WEESPERSTRAAT

Keizersgracht

Wittenberg

Dr Sarphatihuis

Kerkstraat

euwe

Nieuwe

insengracht

Lepelstr

0   250 m

0   250 yds

H   J

Joods Historisch Museum

Silver Hanukkah lamp (left) on display at the Jewish Historical Museum (right)

THE BASICS

jck.nl

🔲 G6

✉ Nieuwe Amstelstraat 1

☎ 531 0310

🕐 Daily 11–5 (Thu until 9). Closed Yom Kippur and Jewish New Year

🍴 Café

Ⓦ Waterlooplein

🚊 Tram 9, 14,

🚌 Hop On-Hop Off stop 3

♿ Very good

💰 Moderate

HIGHLIGHTS

● Grote Synagoge (Great Synagogue, 1671)
● Holy Ark (1791)
● Haggadah Manuscript (1734)

DID YOU KNOW?

● 1597—The first Jew gained Dutch citizenship.
● 112,000 of the 140,000-strong Dutch Jewish community were killed in World War II.

A remarkable exhibition devoted to Judaism tells the story of Jewish settlement in Amsterdam. The most memorable and poignant part portrays the horrors of the Holocaust.

Reconstruction In the heart of what used to be a Jewish area, this complex of four former synagogues is the largest and most important Jewish museum outside Israel. The buildings lay in ruins for many years after World War II and were restored in the 1980s.

Historical exhibits The New Synagogue (1752) gives a lengthy, detailed history of Judaism, with displays of religious objects. The Great Synagogue (1671) is of more general interest, and defines the role of the Jewish community in Amsterdam's trade and industry. Downstairs is a chilling exhibition from the war years and a moving collection by Jewish painters. The remaining two synagogues in the complex are the Obbene Sjoel (1685) and the Dritt Sjoel (1778).

The Dockworker The Nazis occupied Amsterdam in May 1940, and in February 1941, 400 Jews were gathered outside the Great Synagogue by the SS, herded into trucks and taken away. This triggered the February Strike, a general strike led by dockers. Though suppressed after only two days, it was Amsterdam's first open revolt against Nazism and gave impetus to the resistance movement.

The Magere Brug or Skinny Bridge looks attractive illuminated at night

Magere Brug

This traditional double-leaf Dutch drawbridge is a city landmark. At night it is one of the most photographed sights in Amsterdam, illuminated by strings of enchanting lights.

Skinny sisters Of Amsterdam's 1,200 or so bridges, the wooden Skinny Bridge is, without doubt, the best known. On the Amstel river, it is a 20th-century replica of a 17th-century drawbridge. Tradition has it that, in 1670, a simple footbridge was built by two elderly sisters named Mager (meaning skinny), who lived on one side of the Amstel and wanted easy access to their carriage and horses, stabled on the other bank. It seems more likely, however, that the bridge took its name from its narrow girth. In 1772, it was widened and became a double drawbridge, enabling ships of heavy tonnage to sail up the Amstel from the IJ, an inlet of what was then a sea called the Zuiderzee and is now the IJsselmeer, a freshwater lake.

City uproar In 1929, the city council discussed whether to demolish the old frame, which had rotted, and replace it with an electrically operated bridge. After a huge outcry, the people of the city voted overwhelmingly to save the original wooden bridge.

Latest crossing The present bridge, made of African azobe wood, was erected in 1969 and its mechanical drive installed in 1994. Its graceful proportions are still pleasing to the eye.

THE BASICS

✚ G6

✉ At Kerkstraat on the Amstel river

🚇 Waterlooplein

🚃 Tram 4

DID YOU KNOW?

● Around 63,000 boats pass under the bridge each year.
● The rebuilding of the bridge in 1969 cost €63,530.
● There are 66 drawbridges in Amsterdam; 8 are wooden.

THE EAST TOP 25

Museum Het Rembrandthuis

Not always respected during his lifetime, Rembrandt's image and work is everywhere

THE BASICS

rembrandthuis.nl
🔲 G5
✉ Jodenbreestraat 4
☎ 520 0400
🕐 Daily 10–6
Ⓜ Nieuwmarkt, Waterlooplein
🚋 Tram 9, 14
🚌 Hop On-Hop Off stop 2
♿ Few
💵 Expensive
❓ Brief film of Rembrandt's life

HIGHLIGHTS

● *Self-portrait with a Surprised Expression*
● *Five Studies of the Head of Saskia and one of An Older Woman*
● *View of Amsterdam*
● *Christ Shown to the People*

For 20 years, one of the greatest artists in history lived and worked in this historic 17th-century house, now a showcase for his paintings and etchings.

From riches to rags In this red-shuttered canal house, Rembrandt spent the happiest and most successful years of his life, producing many of his most famous paintings and prints. Through his wife, the wealthy heiress Saskia van Uylenburgh, the up-and-coming young artist was introduced to Amsterdam's patrician class and commissions for portraits poured in. He rapidly became an esteemed painter, and bought this large house in 1639 as a symbol of his newfound respectability. Following Saskia's death in 1642, soon after the birth of their son Titus, Rembrandt's work became unfashionable. In 1656, he was declared bankrupt. The house and most of his possessions were sold in 1658, although Rembrandt continued to live here until 1660, when he was obliged to leave. He died a pauper in 1669.

Funny faces Rembrandt's etchings (many of them created in this house) were as important as his painting. In fact, his mastery in this medium inspired its recognition as an art form for the first time. Four of his copper etching plates are on display, together with a series of biblical illustrations. Look out for studies of street figures hung alongside some entertaining self-portraits in various guises, and some mirror images of himself making faces.

Both inside and out, the Willet-Holthuysen museum oozes classical elegance

Museum Willet-Holthuysen

Behind the facade of this beautifully preserved mansion lies a sumptuously furnished home with a delightful garden, a rare luxury in Amsterdam.

Rare insight Standing on Herengracht, Amsterdam's most elegant canal (▷ 44), this house was built in 1687 for Jacob Hop, a wealthy member of the city council. It changed hands many times and eventually, in 1855, came into the possession of a glass merchant named Pieter Gerard Holthuysen. On his death, it became the home of his daughter Sandra and her husband, the art collector Abraham Willet, who together built up a valuable collection of glass, silver, ceramics and paintings. The couple bequeathed the house and its contents to the city in 1895, for use as a museum. Extensively restorated in the late 1990s, the museum provides a rare insight into life in Amsterdam's grand canal houses in the 17th to 19th centuries.

Luxury and grandeur The rooms are decorated with inlaid wood and lacquered panels with painted ceilings. Be sure to see the Blue Room, formerly the preserve of the gentlemen of the house, and the 17th-century kitchen, with its original plumbing. Guests would be served tea in the tiny, octagonal conservatory painted in the customary pale green, overlooking an immaculate French-style formal garden. This rare 18th-century garden is a jewel not to be missed.

THE BASICS

willetholthuysen.nl

- G6
- ✉ Herengracht 605
- ☎ 523 1822
- 🕐 Mon–Fri 10–5, Sat–Sun and public hols 11–5
- Ⓜ Waterlooplein
- 🚋 Tram 4, 9, 14
- 🚌 Hop On-Hop Off stop 3
- ♿ None
- Moderate

HIGHLIGHTS

- Blue Room
- Dining Room
- Porcelain and silver collections
- Kitchen
- Conservatory
- Garden

THE EAST TOP 25

NEMO Science Museum

TIP

- Allow at least three hours to see everything, more with inquisitve children.

The largest science museum in the Netherlands has five floors—and a roof—packed with interactive exhibits, providing both education and fun for children of all ages.

The building The NEMO building is quite an exhibit in itself, looking rather like a huge green ship about to take off into space from its dockside setting. It was designed by the renowned Italian architect Renzo Piano, the man who came up with startling and imaginative ideas for the Pompidou Centre in Paris, the living roof of the California Academy of Sciences in San Francisco and The Shard in London.

The roof The roof is one of the most popular places, as it is more than simply somewhere to

Clockwise from left: The Roof Terrace has become a popular spot; the striking sea-green museum, deliberately designed to look like a ship, is an East Dock landmark; the Science Museum is very hands-on and children are encouraged to have fun with the exhibits

get a good view. An exhibit called Energetica consists of sculptures and installations that you can control yourself in order to harness energy from the wind, water and the sun. Young children will like the surprise fountains and the rainbow maker. The lovely Dak restaurant on the roof can be accessed without purchasing a museum ticket.

Exhibitions inside Soap Bubbles is one of the most popular exhibits inside, where you can not only blow giant bubbles but fit inside them too. Amazing Constructions shows how bridges and buildings work, while The Machine allows you to operate a robotic arm, assemble a product and prepare it for shipping. In the Journey through the Mind exhibit, you can test yourself and learn all about the brain.

THE BASICS

nemosciencemuseum.nl

➕ H4

✉ Oosterdok 2

☎ 531 3233

🕐 Tue–Sun 10–5.30 (also Mon Jun–Aug)

🍴 Café

🚌 Bus 22, 48

🚏 Hop On-Hop Off stop 1, 2

♿ Very good

💶 Expensive

More to See

AMSTEL

The river is a busy commercial thoroughfare, with barges carrying goods to and from the port. In town, its bustling banks are lined by houseboats.

➕ G6 🚊 Tram 3, 7, 9, 10, 12, 14

AMSTELKERK

stadsherstel.nl

Squat and wooden, this Calvinist church (1670) was originally meant to be a temporary structure. During the French occupation of the Netherlands it may have been used by Napoleon who housed his horses inside. It is now mainly used as a concert venue thanks to its excellent acoustics.

➕ F7 ✉ Amstelveld 10 ☎ 520 0090 🕐 Hours vary, call ahead 🚊 Tram 4 ✋ Free

HERMITAGE AMSTERDAM

hermitage.nl

This is a branch of St. Petersburg's Hermitage Museum, which is housed in the 17th-century Amstelhof complex. For years it was an old people's home before being redeveloped into a gallery. Exhibitions are taken from the Russian parent's collection of paintings, sculptures and antiquities.

➕ G6 ✉ Amstelhof, Amstel 51 ☎ 530 7488 🕐 Daily 10–5 🍴 Café 🚇 Waterlooplein 🚊 Tram 9, 14 🚌 Hop On-Hop Off stop 3 ♿ Very good ✋ Expensive

HET SCHEEPVAARTMUSEUM

hetscheepvaartmuseum.nl

The National Maritime Museum showcases Amsterdam's notable history of seafaring, with a fine collection of ships, models and nautical artifacts. Be sure to see the *Amsterdam*, a fascinating and impressive replica of an 18th-century Dutch East Indiaman that sank off the English coast during her maiden voyage in 1749.

➕ J5 ✉ Kattenburgerplein 1 ☎ 523 2222 🕐 Daily 9–5 🍴 Café 🚌 Bus 22, 42, 43 🚌 Hop On-Hop Off stop 2 ♿ Very good ✋ Expensive

National Maritime Museum (above); the Palm House at the Botanical Gardens (left)

HORTUS BOTANICUS

dehortus.nl

With more than 6,000 species, Amsterdam's oldest botanical garden (established in 1638) has one of the largest collections in the world. It has tropical greenhouses, a medicinal herb garden and an orchid nursery.

➕ H6 ✉ Plantage Middenlaan 2a
☎ 625 9021 ⏰ Daily 10–5 🍴 Café
🚋 Tram 9, 14 ♿ Good 💶 Moderate

JODENBUURT

Jewish refugees first settled here in the 16th century. Almost the entire district was razed to the ground at the end of World War II, leaving only a few synagogues (▷ 68), mansions and diamond factories as the legacy of a once-thriving community.

➕ G5 🚇 Waterlooplein

MUSEUM VAN LOON

museumvanloon.nl

The Van Loon family lived in this house during the 19th century,

The garden of the Museum Van Loon

holding important positions as city mayors and in the United East India Company. The house and its collection are in fine condition, as are the coach house and garden. Every year in the third week of June, the museum organizes the Open Garden Days, when private gardens in the city are opened to the public.

➕ F6 ✉ Keizersgracht 672 ☎ 624 5255
⏰ Daily 10–5 🚋 Tram 16 💶 Moderate

NATIONAAL VAKBONDSMUSEUM

deburcht.nl

A museum devoted to trade unions may not sound that appealing but the building is impressive and its grandiose interior full of designs by leading artists of the day. Sunlight streams in through a double roof of yellow and white glass.

➕ H5 ✉ Henri Polaklaan 9 ☎ 624 1166
⏰ Closed for refurbishment; access by booking one of the occasional guided tours
🚋 Tram 9 ♿ Good 💶 Inexpensive

NATIONALE OPERA & BALLET

operaballet.nl

Amsterdam's venue for opera and ballet is affectionately known as the "false teeth" because of its white marble panelling and red-brick roof. The complex includes the buildings of the new city hall (Stadhuis). The design caused great controversy when it was built back in 1986, and its construction in the heart of an "alternative" zone sparked a number of riots. If you're not going to see a concert, there are guided tours, in Dutch, on Saturdays.

➕ G5 ✉ Waterlooplein 22 ☎ 625 5455
🚇 Waterlooplein 🚋 Tram 9, 14

PORTUGESE SYNAGOGE

jck.nl

Holland's finest synagogue, from 1675, was one of the first in Western Europe. It's remarkable that it escaped destruction in World War II.

🔳 G6 ⊠ Mr Visserplein 3 ☎ 624 5351 ⏰ Daily 10–5. Closed Jewish holidays 🚇 Waterlooplein 🚌 Hop On-Hop Off stop 2, 3 🚊 Tram 9, 14 💷 Moderate

REGULIERSGRACHT

Tour boats slow here to give you a view of the seven identical humped bridges stretching along the canal. With their strings of lights, they are best viewed from the water at night.

🔳 F6 🚊 Tram 4, 16

SCHEEPVAARTHUIS

The peculiarly tapered Shipping House suggests the bow of an approaching ship. Commissioned in 1912, it represents an impressive example of Amsterdamse School architecture and is now a hotel.

🔳 G4 ⊠ Prins Hendrikkade 108 🚌 Bus 22, 42, 43

TASSENMUSEUM HENDRIKJE

tassenmuseum.nl

This interesting collection of bags and purses has items dating from the 1500s to the latest fashions.

🔳 F5 ⊠ Herengracht 573 ☎ 524 6452 ⏰ Daily 10–5 🚊 Tram 4, 9 💷 Expensive

VERZETSMUSEUM

verzetsmuseum.org

The Resistance Museum displays rare memorabilia, and the Junior museum is great for younger visitors, as the exhibits are set up as streets during the Nazi occupation.

🔳 H5 ⊠ Plantage Kerklaan 61a ☎ 620 2535 ⏰ Mon–Fri 10–5, Sat–Sun 11–5 🚊 Tram 9, 14 ♿ Good 💷 Expensive

ZUIDERKERK

zuiderkerkamsterdam.nl

Holland's first Protestant church (1611) is beautiful, with an 80m (265ft) tower.

🔳 G5 ⊠ Zuiderkerkhof 72 ☎ 552 7977 ⏰ Mon–Fri 9–5, Sat noon–4; tower Jun–Sep Wed–Sat 2–4 🚇 Nieuwmarkt 💷 Free; tower moderate

The unusually shaped Scheepvaarthuis building

The soaring spire of Zuiderkerk

Shopping

AMSTELVELD PLANTENMARKT

Less famous than the flower market on Singel (▷ 50), the weekly flower and plant market on this Prinsengracht square is more like a normal market.

➕ F7 ✉ Amstelveld 🕐 Mon 9–3 🚋 Tram 4

CONCERTO

concerto.amsterdam

This has the finest all-round selection of new and used records and CDs. Good for jazz, classical music and 1950s and 1960s hits. There's a nice coffee bar inside and spontaneous live musical performances are not uncommon.

➕ G6 ✉ Utrechtsestraat 52–60 ☎ 623 5228 🚋 Tram 4

GASSAN DIAMONDS

gassandiamonds.com

A tour (daily) of the diamond-polishing and cutting workshop leads you, inevitably, to the sales room.

➕ G5 ✉ Nieuwe Uilenburgerstraat 173–175 ☎ 622 5333 🚇 Waterlooplein 🚋 Tram 9, 14

GONE WITH THE WIND

gonewiththewind.nl

Quality toys including German-made Haba wooden baby toys, Swedish-made BRIO train sets, Danish-made Flensted mobiles and fun Dutch souvenirs are this shop's specialty.

➕ F6 ✉ Vijzelstraat 22 ☎ 423 0230 🚋 Tram 4, 9, 14, 16

JASKI GALLERY

jaski.nl

The gallery specializes in painting, sculpture, ceramics and graphic art by the CoBrA artists (1948–1951), including works by Dutch artist Karel Appel. Contemporary artists are also exhibited.

➕ E6 ✉ Nieuwe Spiegelstraat 29 ☎ 620 3939 🚋 Tram 7, 10

DE KLOMPENBOER

woodenshoefactory.com

Bruno the clog-maker no longer does the laborious job of handcarving clogs out of wood, but he does sell a huge selection, decorated in all sorts of colours and patterns.

➕ G5 ✉ Sint-Antoniesbreestraat 39–51 ☎ 427 3862 🚇 Nieuwmarkt

KRAMER KUNST & ANTIEK

antique-tileshop.nl

You'll find a vast collection of vintage Dutch tiles (some from the 1500s), silverware, crystal, clocks, books and paintings at this art and antiques shop.

➕ E6 ✉ Prinsengracht 807 ☎ 626 1116 🚋 Tram 7, 10

PATISSERIE HOLTKAMP

patisserieholtkamp.nl

An art deco storefront is the icing on the cake for a luscious array of patisserie—cakes, tarts, fruit pies and more, including Dutch specialties.

➕ F7 ✉ Vijzelgracht 15 ☎ 624 8757 🚋 Tram 7, 10, 16

REMBRANDT ART MARKET

rembrandtartmarket.nl

Purchase original local art at this elegant market, or simply enjoy the outdoor atmosphere, listening to music.

➕ F6 ✉ Rembrandtplein 🕐 Mar–Oct Sun 10.30–6 🚋 Tram 4, 9, 14

WATERLOOPLEINMARKT

waterlooplein.amsterdam

Amsterdam's liveliest market is full of all sorts: clothes, curiosities, antiques, junk and more. You'll have to sift through a lot of stuff but you may end up finding a treasure for a bargain price.

➕ G5 ✉ Waterlooplein 🕐 Mon–Sat 9.30–6 🚋 Tram 9, 14

Entertainment and Nightlife

BARNEY'S LOUNGE

barneysamsterdam.com

This popular lounge and coffee shop has a nice, quiet canalside location. There are DJs at the weekend, the staff are friendly and helpful, and the milkshakes are highly recommended.

F6 ⊠ Reguliersgracht 27 ☎ 420 6655 🕔 Daily 9.30am–1am 🚊 Tram 4, 9, 14, 16

CAFÉ SCHILLER

cafeschiller.nl

An evocative art deco bar that is enhanced with live piano music. Relax with a good beer and some *bitterballen* (round meat ragu in breadcrumbs) or select from a fuller menu, away from the crowds on Rembrandtplein.

F6 ⊠ Rembrandtplein 24 🕔 Mon–Thu 4pm–1am, Fri 4pm–3am, Sat 1pm–3am, Sun 1pm–1am ☎ 624 9846 🚊 Tram 4, 9, 14

CAFÉ DE SLUYSWACHT

sluyswacht.nl

The rickety 17th-century Sluyswacht building is right on the canal. There are tables outside and a cosy inside bar with wooden tables and beams that is full until the early hours.

G5 ⊠ Jodenbreestraat 1 ☎ 625 7611 🕔 Mon–Thu 12.30pm–1am, Fri–Sat 12.30pm–3am, Sun 12.30pm–7am 🚇 Waterlooplein 🚊 Tram 9, 14

ESCAPE

escape.nl

One of Amsterdam's largest clubs, with a capacity for 2,000 people, Escape has a superb light show and sound system. World-famous DJs have played here including Tiësto, Armin van Buuren and David Guetta.

F6 ⊠ Rembrandtplein 11 ☎ 622 1111 🕔 11pm–4am (Fri–Sat until 5am) 🚊 Tram 4, 9, 14

GREENHOUSE NAMASTE

greenhouse.org

Celebrities like to frequent this popular coffee shop chain, which has four locations around the city. Let the staff know what you are looking for—they are more than happy to help.

G6 ⊠ Waterlooplein 345 ☎ 622 5499 🕔 Daily 9am–1am (Fri–Sat until 2am) 🚇 Waterlooplein 🚊 Tram 9, 14

KONINKLIJK THEATER CARRÉ

carre.nl

The beautiful 19th-century Royal Theatre hosts long-running international musicals, revues, cabaret, folk dancing and an annual World Christmas Circus.

G7 ⊠ Amstel 115–25 ☎ 0900 252 5255 🚇 Weesperplein

DE KROON

dekroon.nl

This restaurant/café/club affects a cool, hard-edged modernity as if to belie a location on the rambunctious Rembrandtplein. The succulent steak dinners are complemented by the well-made cocktails.

F6 ⊠ Rembrandtplein 17 ☎ 625 2011 🕔 Daily 4pm–late 🚊 Tram 4, 9, 14

FILM GUIDE

The city's main multiscreen cinema complexes, in the Leidseplein and Rembrandtplein areas, follow Hollywood's lead closely. The latest big US releases and British films that become international hits are sure to show up on Amsterdam's screens after a short delay. Films from other countries occasionally make it to the city's screens. Almost all films are shown in their original language, with Dutch subtitles; an exception is children's films, which are largely screened in Dutch.

Where to Eat

PRICES	
Prices are approximate, based on a 3-course meal for one person.	
€€€	over €50
€€	€25–€50
€	under €25

BLOEM (€)

bloem36.nl

This casual, pretty café is handy for the zoo. Everything on the menu is organic, including the drinks, and there are great options for vegetarians.

➕ J5 ✉ Entrepotdok 36, Plantage ☎ 330 0929 🕓 Daily 11–9 🚊 Tram 9, 14

BREITNER (€€)

restaurant-breitner.nl

Named after Dutch impressionist George Hendrik Breitner (1857–1923), the romantic view of the Amstel and Herengracht from this charming French restaurant is a fine example of what the artist liked to paint and photograph.

➕ G6 ✉ Amstel 212, Grachtengordel ☎ 627 7879 🕓 Tue–Sat 6–11 🚊 Tram 4, 9, 14

CAFÉ DE FLES (€€)

defles.nl

Mingle with locals at this cellar café while gobbling up savory grilled meats and vegetables. On warm days you'll find plenty of seating along the canal.

➕ F6 ✉ Prinsengracht 955, Grachtengordel ☎ 624 9644 🕓 Mon–Thu 4pm–1am, Fri–Sat 4pm–2am, Sun 3pm–11pm 🚊 Tram 7, 10, 16

CHOUX (€€)

choux.nl

The seasonal New Dutch menu at this modern restaurant give fresh vegetables a leading role. Choose from the set menus and dare to devour the works of art that get put before you. Reservations recommended.

➕ H3 ✉ De Ruyterkade 128, Centrum ☎ 651 2364 🕓 Mon–Fri noon–2pm, Tue–Sat 6pm–10pm 🚊 Tram 4, 9, 16, 26

INDRAPURA (€€)

indrapura.nl

You can tell the waiter how spicy you want your dishes to be at this popular Indonesian restaurant. It serves some of the best *rijsttafel* in town.

➕ F6 ✉ Rembrandtplein 40–42, Rembrandtplein ☎ 623 7329 🕓 Daily 5–10 🚊 Tram 4, 9, 14

LA PLACE (€)

laplace.com

On the top floor of the Openbare Bibliotheek (public library) is a smart café with loads of options at great prices. Choose from sandwiches, salads, noodles, pizza, desserts and smoothies. The terrace has wonderful city views.

➕ H4 ✉ Oosterdokskade 143, Centrum ☎ 523 0870 🕓 Daily 10–10 🚊 Tram 26

SEGUGIO (€€€)

segugio.nl

It's worth splurging at this romantic Italian, with daily fish, risotto and soup specials, but leave room for the superb *zabaione* and a glass of grappa.

➕ G7 ✉ Utrechtsestraat 96, Grachtengordel ☎ 330 1503 🕓 Mon–Sat 6–11 🚊 Tram 4

TEMPO DOELOE (€€)

tempodoeloerestaurant.nl

Reservations are required at this neat and elegant Indonesian restaurant. It's been a local favourite for years and has an impressive wine list too. Be warned: spicy really does mean spicy here.

➕ G6 ✉ Utrechtsestraat 75, Grachtengordel ☎ 625 6718 🕓 Mon–Sat 6–12 🚊 Tram 4

Museum District

This important cultural area, with its museums celebrating Amsterdam's best-known artists, is a distinct district set apart from the city's old quarter, close to the main city park.

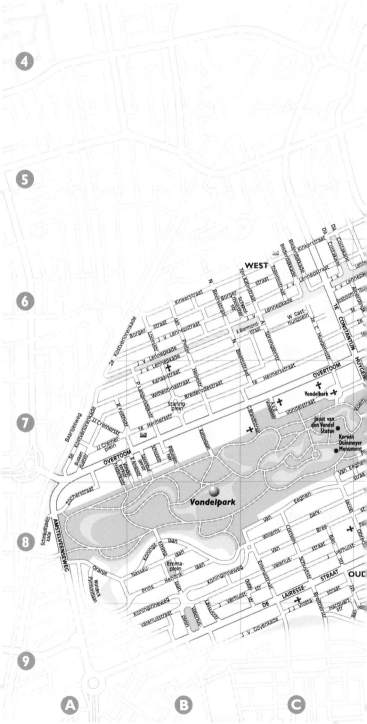

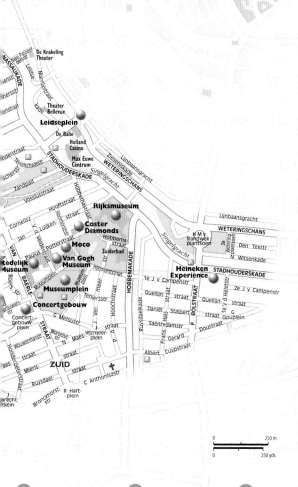

De Krakeling
Theater

Theater
Bellevue
Leidseplein
De Balie
Holland
Casino
Max Euwe
Centrum

NASSAUKADE

Nieuwe Passeer...
derssr
Leidse...
Marnixstraat
...nerstr
kade
...erstraat

...delstraat
...selsschadestr
...scherstr
Zandbad

STADHOUDERSKADE
Ziezenisskade
Lijnbaansgracht
WETERINGSCHANS
Singelgracht

Vosslusstraat
Hooftstraat
Hobbemakade

Rijksmuseum
Cornelisz
Jan
**Coster
Diamonds**
Hobbema-
straat
Lijnbaansgracht
WETERINGSCHANS
H.M.V.
Randwijk-
plantsoen
2e Wetering plantsoen
Den Texstr

Paulus Potterstr
Moco
Zuiderbad

...tedelijk
useum
**Van Gogh
Museum**
VAN
BAERLE
Museumbrug
HOBBEMAKADE

Hoofdstraat
**Heineken
Experience**
STADHOUDERSKADE
N. Witsenkade
Singelgracht

Boek...
Museumplein
Teniersstr
Museumplein
1e J v Campenstr
2e J v Campenstr

...rouwers
Concertgebouw
Concert-
gebouw-
plein
C. Metsustr
Ver... meer
Hooghstraat
Quellijn- straat
Quellijn- straat
G
Douplein

Wouwermanstr
STRAAT
Moreelse-
str
Frans Hals
Daniel Stalpert straat
Saenredamstr
Gerard
Doustraat

...aes Mieris
ZUID
N. Maes
straat
Vermeer-
plein
Albert Cuypstraat

Ruysdael-
straat
C. Anthoniszstr

Bronckhorst-
str
R Hart-
plein

...recht-
...lein

0 — 250 m
0 — 250 yds

Ⓓ   Ⓔ   Ⓕ

Leidseplein

TOP **25**

Amsterdam's liveliest square is busy both night and day

THE BASICS

➕ E6
✉ Leidseplein
🍴 Restaurants and cafés
🚋 Tram 1, 2, 5, 7, 10, 16
🚌 Hop On–Hop Off stop 5

HIGHLIGHTS

● American Hotel (1904)
● Stadsschouwburg (1894)
● Street entertainment

This square represents Amsterdam's nightlife at its most vibrant. It is filled with street cafés, ablaze with neon and abuzz with street entertainers.

Party district for centuries During the Middle Ages, farmers on their way to market unloaded their carts here, at the outskirts of the city. At the turn of the 19th century, artists and writers gathered here. In the 1930s, Leidseplein was the site of many clashes between political factions, and it became the main site of anti-Nazi rallies during the war. In the 1960s, it was the stomping ground of the *Pleiners* (Dutch Mods). Today, despite the constant flow of trams through the square, you are almost sure to find fire-eaters and other street entertainers, both good and bad. By night, dazzling neon lights and crowded café terraces seating more than 1,000 people transform the square into an Amsterdam hotspot, busy until the early hours. Look for two notable buildings, both protected monuments: the distinctive redbrick Stadsschouwburg (Municipal Theatre, ▷ 93), with its wide veranda and little turrets, and the art nouveau Hampshire Hotel Amsterdam American (▷ 112), with its striking art deco Café Americain (▷ 94).

Winter wonderland Whatever the season, Leidseplein remains one of the city's main meeting places. In winter, when most tourists have departed, it becomes quintessentially Dutch, complete with a little skating rink.

Designed by Pierre Cuypers in 1885, this is the place to view the famous Night Watch

TOP 25

Rijksmuseum

The Rijksmuseum's masterpieces are a glorious evocation of the Dutch Golden Age of the 17th century, with key works by Rembrandt and Vermeer.

Old Masters The Rijksmuseum is the major national art gallery of the Netherlands, with more than one million items in its collections. After 10 years of partial closure, it triumphantly reopened in April 2013 complete with new state-of-the-art lighting system, which uses 750,000 LED lights to simulate natural daylight. The highlight is still the separate room in which the single most important work in the Rijksmuseum, Rembrandt's *The Night Watch*, is displayed to great effect. This monumental canvas is so huge and powerful it will stop you in your tracks. The other great Dutch name in the collection is Johannes Vermeer. The most familiar of his works is probably *The Milkmaid*, a beautifully lit portrait of a young woman pouring milk into a bowl. Other Dutch masters from this period include Jan Steen, Frans Hals and Aelbert Cuyp, but there is also modern art from Karel Appel among others, and an impressive collection of wonderful Delftware porcelain.

Design masterpiece Don't limit yourself to the art collection—admire the museum's architecture too. The palatial redbrick building was designed by Pierre Cuypers and opened in 1885. It is mostly in the style known as Dutch neo-Renaissance, but Cuypers managed to slip in some neo-Gothic touches.

THE BASICS

rijksmuseum.nl
🔢 E7
✉ Museumstraat 1
☎ 674 7000
🕐 Daily 9–5
🍴 Restaurant and café
🚊 Tram 2, 3, 5, 7, 10, 12, 16
🚌 Hop On-Hop Off stop 5
♿ Very good
✋ Expensive

HIGHLIGHTS

● *The Night Watch*, Rembrandt (1642)
● *The Jewish Bride*, Rembrandt (1665)
● *The Milkmaid*, Vermeer (1658)
● *The Love Letter*, Vermeer (1670)
● 17th-century dollhouses

MUSEUM DISTRICT TOP 25

Stedelijk Museum

Outside the museum (left); Wall Painting (Karel Appel, 1956; right)

© Karel Appel Foundation

THE BASICS

stedelijk.nl

🔢 D4

✉ Museumplein 10

☎ 573 2911

🕙 Daily 10–6 (Fri until 10)

🍴 Restaurant

🚊 Tram 2, 3, 5, 7, 10, 12, 16

🚌 Hop On-Hop Off stop 5

♿ Good

💷 Expensive

❷ Lectures, films and concerts

HIGHLIGHTS

● *The Parakeet and the Mermaid,* Matisse (1952–53)

● *My Name as Though it were Written on the Surface of the Moon,* Nauman (1968)

● *Sitting Woman with Fish Hat,* Picasso (1942)

● *Wall Painting Restaurant Stedelijk,* Karel Appel (1956)

● *Beanery,* Kienholz (1965)

● Rietveld furniture collection

This leading modern art museum features work by artists ranging from Henri Matisse to Kazimir Malevich and Piet Mondrian, and Paul Klee to Vasily Kandinsky and Edward Kienholz.

Controversial The Stedelijk or Municipal Museum, was founded in 1895. In recent years, its home base at Museumplein has been extensively refurbished and expanded, greatly increasing the display area and improving access and visibility for visitors. Its collection of more than 90,000 paintings, sculptures, drawings, graphics and photographs contains works by some of the great names of modern art (van Gogh, Cézanne, Picasso, Monet, Chagall), but the emphasis is on progressive postwar movements.

House of Museums In 1938, the Stedelijk became Holland's National Museum of Modern Art, but it achieved its worldwide reputation between 1945–63, when it was under the dynamic direction of Willem Sandberg. He put much of its existing collection in storage and created a House of Museums in which all the arts were represented in innovative shows.

Cutting edge Museum highlights include supramatist paintings by Malevich; works by Mondrian, Gerrit Rietveld and other exponents of the Dutch De Stijl school; and a remarkable collection of almost childlike paintings by the members of CoBrA movement.

*The Vondelpark
Pavillion (left); the
park is perfect for
relaxation (right)*

Vondelpark

This is a popular place for sunbathers, joggers, frisbee-throwers and book-worms. Be entertained by street players and acrobats in this welcome splash of green near the heart of the city.

Pleasure gardens With its wide-open spaces, fragrant rose garden, playgrounds, bandstand and cafés, Vondelpark is a popular place to relax. Amsterdam's largest and oldest municipal park—a 48-hectare (118-acre) rectangle of former marshland—was first opened in 1865. The designers, J.D. and L.P. Zocher, created an English landscape-style park with lengthy path-ways, open lawns, ornamental lakes, meadows and woodland containing 120 varieties of tree. Financed by wealthy local residents, the Nieuwe Park (New Park, as it was then called) became the heart of a luxurious new residential district, overlooked by elegant villas. Two years later, a statue of Holland's best-known playwright, Joost van den Vondel (1587–1679) was erected in the park. There is also a Picasso statue: *The Fish*. It is the only city park in Holland that has been designated a listed monument.

Like a summer-long festival The heyday of Vondelpark was in the 1970s, when people flocked to Amsterdam, attracted by the city's tolerance for soft drugs. Vondelpark soon became the main gathering place. The bubble burst at the end of the decade and the people left. All that remains of the spirit of that time are street musicians and flea markets.

THE BASICS

➕ B8
✉ Stadhouderskade
🕐 Dawn–dusk
🍴 Groot Melkhuis (▷ 94), 't Blauwe Theehuis (▷ 92)
🚊 Tram 1, 2, 3, 5, 12
🚌 Hop On-Hop Off stop 5
♿ Good
❓ Open-air summer festival of plays and concerts

DID YOU KNOW?

● Vondelpark was originally built on peat, just like the rest of the city. Unlike most of the buildings however, the park lacks a foundation and has been slowly sinking for the last 150 or more years. It is now lying two metres lower than its surroundings. Recently, the city has been restoring the park and improving the drainage system. Special foundations have been laid under the trees to protect them from sinking too far.

MUSEUM DISTRICT TOP 25

Van Gogh Museum

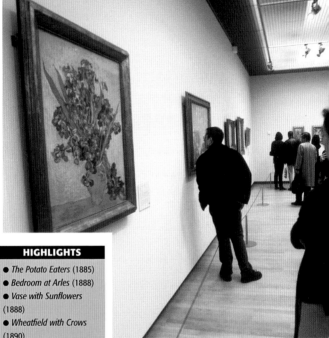

HIGHLIGHTS

- *The Potato Eaters* (1885)
- *Bedroom at Arles* (1888)
- *Vase with Sunflowers* (1888)
- *Wheatfield with Crows* (1890)
- *Sunset at Montmajour* (1888)

TIPS

- Book your tickets online to avoid long lines.
- It's well worth getting the audio guide for an extra fee.

DID YOU KNOW?

- Van Gogh sold only one painting in his lifetime.
- The record price for a Van Gogh painting is €56 million (1990, *Portrait of Dr. Gachet*).

It is a moving experience to trace Vincent van Gogh's tragic life and extraordinary achievement through such a varied display of his art.

World's largest collection The museum has 200 of Van Gogh's paintings and 500 of his drawings, together with 850 letters, his fine Japanese prints and works by friends and contemporaries, including Gauguin, Monet, Emile, Bernard and Pissarro. Van Gogh's paintings are arranged chronologically, starting with works from 1880 to 1887.

Artist's palette The brush strokes and bold tones that characterize Van Gogh's works from 1887 to 1890 show the influence of his 1886 move to Paris and the effect of

People come from all over to view the most famous pictures by Vincent van Gogh, including Irises *(left); the museum houses the largest collection of Van Gogh's work anywhere in the world and the building has been specially designed to accommodate his art (right)*

Impressionism, most striking in street and café scenes. Tired of city life, he moved in 1888 to Arles where, intoxicated by the intense sunlight and the brilliant hues of Provence, he painted many of his finest works, including *Harvest at La Crau* and the Sunflowers series. After snipping off a bit of his ear and offering it to a local prostitute, Van Gogh voluntarily entered an asylum in St.-Rémy, where his art took an expressionistic form. His mental anguish may be seen in the way he painted gnarled trees and menacing skies, as in the desolate *Wheatfield with Crows*. At the age of 37, he took his own life.

Extra space Temporary and special exhibitions are mounted in an elliptical wing designed by architect Kisho Kurokawa.

More to See

COSTER DIAMONDS

costerdiamonds.com

The diamond business has flourished in Amsterdam since the 16th century. This quality diamond workshop is one of only a few in the city to give tours, and you'll see diamond cutters at work.

D7 Paulus Potterstraat 2–8 305 5555 Daily 9–5 Tram 2, 5 Few Free

HEINEKEN EXPERIENCE

heineken.com

An introduction to the world of Heineken beer can be found in the former brewery, a building that was producing beer until 1988. You'll learn about brewing and see old Heineken adverts. Don't miss the stables housing the shire horses that are still used to pull the promotional drays around Amsterdam.

F8 Stadhouderskade 78 523 9222 Mon–Thu 10.30–7.30, Fri–Sun 10.30–9 (last entry 2 hours before closing) Tram 4, 6, 7, 10, 16 Few (call in advance) Expensive

MOCO

mocomuseum.com

The compact but fascinating Modern Contemporary Museum Amsterdam exhibits artists such as Warhol, Dali and Banksy inside a converted, quirky old house.

D7 Honthorstraat 20 370 1997 Daily 10–6 Tram 2, 5, 16 Expensive

MUSEUMPLEIN

This large, irregularly shaped square was first laid out in 1883 and drastically rearranged in 1999. It is bordered by the Rijksmuseum (▷ 85), the Van Gogh Museum (▷ 88–89) and the Stedelijk Museum (▷ 86). A rectangular pond (and winter ice-skating rink) reflects the surrounding buildings and trees at one end, and at the other is the Concertgebouw. Picnicking and impromptu games of soccer, basketball and pétanque are popular activities.

D8 Museumplein Tram 2, 3, 5, 12, 16, 24 Hop On-Hop Off stop 5

The Concertgebouw on the Museumplein

Around the Museums and the Park

This walk enables you to visit some of the most famous museums in the city and also gives you the chance to relax in the park.

DISTANCE: 3km (2 miles) **ALLOW:** 1–2 hours (plus stops)

START

RIJKSMUSEUM
⊞ E7 🚊 Tram 2, 5, 16

1 Start at the park at the back of the Rijksmuseum (▷ 85) by the museum shop. Across the road is Paulus Potterstraat and Coster Diamonds (▷ 90), where you can take a tour.

2 Continuing along Paulus Potterstraat you will see the Van Gogh Museum (▷ 88–89) and the Stedelijk Museum (▷ 86) on your left. Continue and turn right into Van Baerlestraat.

3 Take the first entrance into the Vondelpark (▷ 87), in front of you. Wander through the park and you will see the statue of Joost van den Vondel.

4 Make your way back to the original entrance. Continue round the park, passing the listed 19th-century pavilion (▷ 93).

END

RIJKSMUSEUM
⊞ E7 🚊 Tram 2, 5, 16

8 Continue to the junction with Hobbemastraat, where the tram rails cross, and you will find the Rijksmuseum at the end.

7 Turn first right onto the main street 1e Constantijn Huygensstraat and take the third left into Pieter Cornelisz Hooftstraat, one of the most exclusive shopping streets in the city; everything from Gucci to Armani is here.

6 This church, reminiscent of Sleeping Beauty's castle, was built in 1880. About 100m (100 yards) to the left of the church is the indoor riding school, the Hollandsche Manege. Retrace your steps and head down Vondelstraat.

5 Leaving the park by the entrance on the right, head to the Vondelkerk ahead of you.

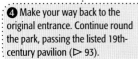

Shopping

BLENDER

blenderamsterdam.nl

This kids' shop and café offers respite from sightseeing with its little indoor playground and toys for young ones to enjoy, while adults treat themselves to coffee and snacks. Clothing and gifts are available for purchase too.

➕ E8 ✉ Ruysdaelstraat 9–11–13 ☎ 845 2615 🚋 Tram 3, 5, 12, 16

BONEBAKKER

bonebakker.nl

A jeweller since 1792, Adrianus Bonebakker made silver keys of the city for Napoleon in 1811 and made the royal crown for King Willem II in 1840, a crown still used by the Dutch Royal family today. Come here for that exquisite piece, if you have the means.

➕ D7 ✉ Van Baerlestraat 27 ☎ 673 7577 🚋 Tram 3, 12

GOOD GENES

thegoodgenes.com

The Dutch love their jeans. Here you'll find locally designed, high quality denim on sale in an exposed-brick studio and shop.

➕ E8 ✉ Albert Cuypstraat 33–35 ☎ 308 0688 🚋 Tram 3, 12, 16

TERRA INCOGNITA

A curio shop filled with unusual gemstones, fossils, meteorites, antiquities and souvenirs that make interesting gifts. The owners are informative and welcoming.

➕ D8 ✉ Van Baerlestraat 77 ☎ 673 8393 🚋 Tram 3, 5, 12, 16

Entertainment and Nightlife

'T BLAUWE THEEHUIS

blauwetheehuis.nl

This 1930s' pagoda-like structure is a popular lunch spot and a great place to people-watch. On Friday evenings during the summer, the stylish upstairs bar features a DJ.

➕ B8 ✉ Vondelpark 5 ☎ 662 0254 🚋 Tram 1, 3, 12

BULLDOG PALACE

thebulldog.com

Flagship of the Bulldog chain of bars and smoking coffee shops, the Palace sells more draft beer than anywhere else in the city. Downstairs is the smoking coffee shop. Mondays, Tuesdays, and Thursdays are karaoke nights.

➕ E6 ✉ Leidseplein 15 ☎ 627 1908 🚋 Tram 1, 2, 5, 6, 7, 10

C'EST MAGNIFIQUE

cest-magnifique.nl

This café has a simple menu of soups, sandwiches and coffee, but its appeal is that it's open from early in the morning (7am) till late at night (4am) and serves the best croissants in town.

➕ E6 ✉ Leidsestraat 18 ☎ 422 7014 🚋 Tram 1, 2, 5

CONCERTGEBOUW

concertgebouw.nl

The magnificent neoclassical Concertgebouw has amazing acoustics, making it special with musicians

worldwide. Since its début in 1888, it has come under the baton of Richard Strauss, Mahler, Ravel, Schönberg and Bernard Haitink to name a few. It continues to be one of the most respected ensembles in the world, attracting renowned performers.

⊞ D8 ⊠ Concertgebouwplein 10 ☎ 671 8345 🚋 Tram 3, 5, 12, 16

HOLLAND CASINO AMSTERDAM

hollandcasino.nl

Try all the usual games, plus sic bo (a Chinese dice game) at this huge casino. There is a small entrance fee, and you must be over 18 and show your passport, but there is no strict dress code.

⊞ D6 ⊠ Max Euweplein 62 ☎ 521 1111 🚋 Tram 1, 2, 5, 7, 10

MELKWEG

melkweg.nl

Located in a wonderful old dairy building (hence the name Melkweg or "Milky Way") on a canal just off Leidseplein, this offbeat multimedia entertainment complex opened in the 1960s and remains a shrine to alternative culture. Live bands play in the old warehouse most evenings, and there is also a schedule of unconventional theatre, dance, art and film events.

⊞ D6 ⊠ Lijnbaansgracht 234 ☎ 531 8181 🚋 Tram 7, 10, 16

PARADISO

paradiso.nl

Housed in an old church, this club has been a rock and pop venue and cultural centre since the 1960s. A number of international musicians have held concerts here, including Adele and the Rolling Stones.

⊞ E7 ⊠ Weteringschans 6–8 ☎ 626 4521 🚋 Tram 7, 10

STADSSCHOUWBURG

stadsschouwburgamsterdam.nl

Classical and modern plays make up the bulk of the repertoire at this stylish, 19th-century municipal theatre. The on-site Café & Brasserie Stanislavski is a beautiful spot for lunch, dinner or a cocktail.

⊞ E6 ⊠ Leidseplein 26 ☎ 624 2311 🚋 Tram 1, 2, 5, 7, 10

VAN GOGH MUSEUM

vangoghmuseum.nl

An unexpected nightlife venue, the Van Gogh Museum lets its hair down from 7pm to 10pm every Friday, with special acts once a month. A DJ plays music, there's a cocktail bar, talks or workshops, and free guided tours of the museum (reserve ahead for these as spaces are limited). If you want to eat too, the museum café stays open, serving tasty, inexpensive meals.

⊞ D7 ⊠ Museumplein 6 ☎ 570 5200 🚋 Tram 2, 3, 5, 7, 10, 12, 16

VONDELPARK OPENLUCHTTHEATER

openluchttheater.nl

This open-air venue in the park offers free drama, cabaret, concerts and children's activities from May to September.

⊞ B3 ⊠ Vondelpark ☎ 428 3360 🚋 Tram 1, 2, 3, 5, 12

ZUIDERBAD

amsterdam.nl

This historic indoor pool (built 1912) is only a short stroll from the Rijksmuseum and is the perfect place for children to enjoy letting off steam as light relief after all that sightseeing. They also offer nude swimming on Sunday evenings.

⊞ E7 ⊠ Hobbemastraat 26 ☎ 252 1390 🚋 Tram 2, 5

Where to Eat

PRICES

Prices are approximate, based on a 3-course meal for one person.

€€€ over €50
€€ €25–€50
€ under €25

BRASSERIE KEYZER (€€)

brasseriekeyzer.nl

An Amsterdam institution for musicians for more than 100 years, Keyzer is right next door to the Concertgebouw. Seafood and French and Dutch specialties are on the menu, and the large covered patio is a comfortable spot to sip a glass of wine.

➕ D8 ✉ Van Baerlestraat 96, Oud Zuid ☎ 675 1866 🕔 Daily 10am–11pm 🚋 Tram 2, 3, 5, 12, 16

CAFÉ AMERICAIN (€)

cafeamericain.nl

Artists, writers and bohemians have frequented this grand art deco café since it opened in 1902. Try the classic afternoon tea, which is served daily from 2pm to 5pm, or the Sunday jazz brunch when there's a buffet and live music (on the first Sunday of each month, except for July and August).

➕ D6 ✉ Hampshire Hotel Amsterdam American, Leidsekade 97 ☎ 556 3010 🕔 Daily 7am–1am 🚋 Tram 1, 2, 5, 7, 10

CAFÉ LOETJE (€€)

loetje.com

Being the original 1970s' location of what is now a chain, this café is still one of the better neighbourhood pubs in the city. The steaks are excellent and the atmosphere is cheerful and laid back.

➕ E8 ✉ Johannes Vermeerstraat 52, Oud Zuid ☎ 662 8173 🕔 Daily 10am–10.30pm 🚋 Tram 3, 5, 12

FOODHALLEN (€)

foodhallen.nl

A former tram depot turned modern indoor food court with a wide range of appealing options, from *bitterballen* to tacos, dim sum and chicken tikka.

➕ C6 ✉ Bellamyplein 51, Oud-West ☎ 218 1775 🕔 Daily 11am–11.30pm, Fri-Sat till 1am 🚋 Tram 7, 17

GROOT MELKHUIS (€€)

grootmelkhuis.nl

This family-friendly café inside the Vondelpark features a large playground and a kid-pleasing menu. They even have a Kids' Art Club on Wednesday afternoons.

➕ B8 ✉ Vondelpark 2 ☎ 612 9674 🕔 Daily 10am–late 🚋 Tram 1, 3, 12

THE SEAFOOD BAR (€€)

theseafoodbar.com

A must for seafood lovers, this is a white-tiled, modern spot right by Vondelpark and quite reasonably priced. The *fruits de mer* is always a good choice, as is the more modest fish and chips.

➕ D7 ✉ Van Baerlestraat 5, Oud-Zuid ☎ 670 8355 🕔 Daily 12–12 (kitchen closes at 10pm) 🚋 Tram 2, 3, 5, 12, 16

A BITE TO "EET"

Try an *eetcafé* for filling, home-made fare, such as soup, sandwiches and omelettes. Kitchens tend to close around 9pm. Most bars offer *borrelhapjes* (mouthfuls with a glass)—usually olives, chunks of cheese or *borrelnoten* (nuts with a tasty coating). More substantial *borrelhapjes* are *bitterballen,* round versions of the *kroket* (meat ragu rolled in breadcrumbs and deep-fried), and *vlammetjes* (spicy mini spring rolls).

Just a bus or tram ride will take you into the suburbs where there's a plethora of windmills, the zoo and more museums. A little farther out it is easy to get to Delft or Keukenhof.

DISTELWEG

JOHAN VAN

NIEUWE LEEUWARDERWEG

NOORD

HASSELTWEG

IJ - TUNNEL

EYE
Film
Museum

Het IJ

DE RUIJTERKADE

CENTRAAL
STATION

PIET HEINKADE

IJhaven

PRINS

Dijksgracht

DAMRAK

Oosterdok

CENTRUM

HENDRIKKADE

KATTENBURGERSTRAAT

Wittenburgervaart

AMSTERDAM

IJ-TUNNEL

Nieuwevaart

Museum
't Kromhout

AMSTEL

WATERLOO
-PLEIN

Entrepotdok

De Gooyer

Hortus
Botanicus

Natura
Artis
Magistra

Artis

PLANTAGE
MIDDENLAAN

MAURITSKADE

WEESPERSTRAAT

Tropenmuseum

LINNAEUSSTRAAT

Singelgracht

Oosterpark

MAURITSKADE

OOST

Amstel

Albert
Cuypmarkt

WIBAUTSTRAAT

arphatipark

WOUSTRAAT

DE PIJP

AMSTELDIJK

NOBELWEG

0   500 m
0   500 yds

RUIJNSTRAAT

GOOISEWEG

Tropenmuseum

TOP 25

Exhibits from the far-flung corners of the earth are on show at the Tropenmuseum

THE BASICS

tropenmuseum.nl

🟦 K7

✉ Linnaeusstraat 2

☎ 568 8200

🕐 Tue–Sun 10–5 (also Mon in school holidays)

🍴 Café De Tropen

🚊 Tram 3, 7, 9, 10, 14

♿ Very good

💰 Expensive

HIGHLIGHTS

- Bombay slums
- Arabian souk
- Bangladeshi village
- Indonesian farmhouse
- Indonesian *gamelan* orchestra
- Pacific carved wooden boats
- Papua New Guinean Bisj Poles
- Puppet collection

In the extraordinary Tropical Museum, once a hymn to colonialism, vibrant reconstructions of street scenes with sounds, photographs and slides evoke contemporary life in tropical regions.

Foundations In 1859, Frederik Willem van Eeden, a member of the Dutch Society for the Promotion of Industry, was asked to establish a collection of objects from the Dutch colonies "for the instruction and amusement of the Dutch people". The collection started with a simple bow, arrows and quiver from Borneo and a lacquer water scoop from Palembang, then expanded at a staggering rate, as did the number of visitors. In the 1920s, to house the collection, the palatial Colonial Institute was constructed and adorned with stone friezes to reflect Holland's imperial achievements. In the 1970s, the emphasis shifted away from the glories of colonialism towards an explanation of issues being faced by these countries. Beside the museum is Oosterpark, a pleasant green space and good spot to relax.

Another world The precious collections are not displayed in glass cases, but set out in lifelike settings, amid evocative sounds, photographs and slide presentations, so that you feel as if you've stepped into other continents. Explore a Bombay slum, feel the fabrics in an Arabian souk, have a rest in a Nigerian bar, meditate in a Hindu temple or listen to the sounds of Latin America in a café.

More to See

1100 ROE

molens.nl

This old smock mill, shaped like a peasant's smock, stands 1,100 roes from the city's outer canal. The word *roe* means both the flat part of a sail that has to be set or reefed according to wind strength, and a unit of measurement (working out at about about 28cm or 1ft) used to calculate the distance from the heart of the city.

➕ See map ▷ 96 ✉ Herman Bonpad 6 🚌 Bus 61

1200 ROE

molens.nl

This early 17th-century post mill, with its impressive platform and revolving cap, was built to drain the polders (a piece of low-lying land reclaimed from the water by building dikes and drainage canals). Although the mill has been restored, it's not functional and now serves as someone's home. You can still take photos of the exterior and walk around it.

➕ See map ▷ 96 ✉ Haarlemmerweg 701 at Willem Molengraaffstraat 🚌 Bus 69

ALBERT CUYPMARKT

albertcuyp-markt.amsterdam

The country's biggest, best-known and least expensive market, named after a Dutch landscape artist, attracts some 20,000 bargain hunters on busy days. Browse the goods of 260 vendors, including many selling tasty snacks.

➕ F8 ✉ Albert Cuypstraat 🕐 Mon–Sat 9–5 🚋 Tram 4, 16

AMSTELPARK

A formal rose garden and a rhodo-dendron valley are two spectacles at this magnificent park, created in 1972 for an international horticultural exhibition. It also offers pony rides, miniature golf, a children's farm, the Rieker windmill (▷ 101) and other attractions. In summer, you can take a tour of the park in a miniature train.

➕ See map ▷ 96 🕐 Daily dawn–dusk 🍴 Restaurant and café ♿ Good 🚋 Tram 4

Sculling down the lake in the Amsterdamse Bos, ▷ 100

AMSTERDAMSE BOS

Amsterdam's largest park was built outside the city in the 1930s. It is a popular weekend destination. In winter, you can go tobogganing and skating, in summer swimming, sailing and biking. You can also take a tram ride through part of the park.

➕ See map ▷ 96 ✉ Amstelveen seweg ⏰ Daily dawn–dusk. Visitor area daily 12–5 🍴 Various cafés and restaurants 🚌 Bus 170, 172

ARTIS

artis.nl

Amsterdam's famous zoo in De Plantage neighbourhood first opened its gates in 1838 and is one of the oldest zoos in Europe. There are close to 800 species of animals here, including elephants, tigers, chimpanzees and penguins. The butterfly house, aquarium and planetarium are great for rainy days.

➕ J6 ✉ Plantage Kerklaan 38–40 ☎ 0900 278 4796 ⏰ Daily 9–5 (summer until 6) 🍴 Restaurant and café 🚋 Tram 9, 10, 14 ♿ Good 💶 Very expensive

COBRA MUSEUM

cobra-museum.nl

Vividly expressionistic works by post-war CoBrA group (Copenhagen, Brussels, Amsterdam) artists Karel Appel, Asger Jorn, Pierre Alechinsky and others are on display here.

➕ See map ▷ 96 ✉ Sandbergplein 1, Amstelveen ☎ 547 5050 ⏰ Tue–Sun 11–5 🚋 Tram 5 ♿ Excellent 💶 Moderate

EYE FILM MUSEUM

eyefilm.nl

The EYE Film Museum, in a striking white building across the harbour from Centraal Station, tells the history of cinema in the Netherlands.

➕ G2 ✉ IJpromenade 1 ☎ 589 1400 ⏰ Daily 10–7 🚌 Bus 38 ⛴ Buiksloterweg ferry from Centraal Station ♿ Good 💶 Free; charge for movies and exhibitions

DE GOOYER

brouwerijhetij.nl

Built on a brick base in 1725, with an octagonal body and a thatched wooden frame, this former flour

Make friends with the fish at Artis Zoo

windmill sits next to the Brouwerij 't IJ–a microbrewery that offers tours and tastings.

🞧 K6 ⊠ Funenkade 5 ⊙ Brewery tours in English Fri–Sun 3.30 🚋 Tram 10 💶 Moderate (brewery tour)

MOLEN VAN SLOTEN

molenvansloten.nl

The functional Sloten Windmill is the only windmill open to the public in Amsterdam. You can view an audiovisual presentation on Rembrandt and a barrel-making exhibit. Guided tours are available.

🞧 See map ▷ 96 ⊠ Akersluis 10 ☎ 669 0412 ⊙ Daily 10–5 🦽 Good 🚋 Tram 2; bus 145 💶 Moderate

MUSEUM 'T KROMHOUT

machinekamer.nl

This living museum documents the development of the Eastern Islands' shipbuilding industry. Ship repairs still take place here.

🞧 J5 ⊠ Hoogte Kadijk 147 ☎ 627 6777 ⊙ Opening times vary, call ahead 🚌 Bus 22, 43 🦽 Few 💶 Moderate

DE PIJP

This lively, multicultural area was once one of Amsterdam's most attractive working-class districts outside the Grachtengordel. The bustling Albert Cuypmarkt takes place daily (▷ 99).

🞧 F8 🚋 Tram 3, 4, 12

DE RIEKER

The finest windmill in Amsterdam, built in 1636 to drain the Rieker polder, stands at the southern tip of Amstelpark. This was one of Rembrandt's special painting locations. The windmill is now a private home.

🞧 See map ▷ 96 ⊠ Amsteldijk, at De Borcht 10 🚌 Bus 62

SARPHATIPARK

This small green oasis is dedicated to 19th-century Jewish doctor and city benefactor Samuel Sarphati. The park has several ponds, a playground and a large monument dedicated to Sarphati.

🞧 F8 ⊙ Daily 9–dusk 🚋 Tram 3, 25

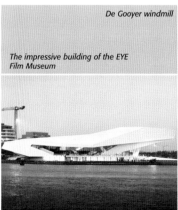

De Gooyer windmill

The impressive building of the EYE Film Museum

Excursions

THE BASICS

Distance: 55km (34 miles) southwest
Journey time: 1 hour
🚆 Train from Amsterdam Centraal Station to Delft
ℹ️ Kerkstraat 3
☎ 015/215 4051; delft.nl
Nieuwe Kerk
oudeennieuwekerkdelft.nl
🕐 Mon–Sat 9–6
💶 Moderate
Oude Kerk
oudeennieuwekerkdelft.nl
🕐 Mon–Sat 9–6
💶 Moderate
Koninklijke Porcelyne Fles
royaldelft.com
🕐 Mon–Sat 9–5, Sun noon–5
💶 Expensive

DELFT

This charming old town is known the world over for its blue-and-white pottery. In 1652, there were 32 thriving potteries; today there are just four.

Birthplace of the painter Jan Vermeer (1632–75) and burial place of Dutch royalty, Delft is a handsome, canal-lined town. Few of its medieval buildings survived a great fire in 1536 and a massive explosion at a powder magazine in 1654. William I of Orange (William the Silent) led his revolt against Spanish rule from the Prinsenhof in Delft. The building now houses the city museum, which includes a collection of rare antique Delftware. William is among the members of the House of Oranje-Nassau who have been buried in the 14th-century Gothic Nieuwe Kerk, Holland's royal church. In addition, you can climb the tower of the New Church, which is 109m (357ft) high, for marvellous views over Delft. Vermeer is buried in the nearby 13th-century Gothic Oude Kerk, which has fine stained-glass windows.

You can visit the workshop of De Koninklijke Porceleyne Fles (Royal Delft), renowned makers of traditional, hand-painted Delft Blue porcelain. A multimedia experience tells the story of Delft porcelain, and naturally there is a chance to buy.

THE BASICS

Distance: 26km (16 miles) southwest
Journey time: 1 hour
🚆 Train from Centraal Station to Leiden then bus direct
✉️ Lisse
☎ 0252 465555; keukenhof.nl
💶 Expensive

KEUKENHOF GARDENS

These gardens—whose name means "kitchen garden"—at the heart of the Bloembollenstreek (bulb-growing region) rank among the most famous in the world. The showcase site was bought in 1949 by a consortium of bulb-growers who saw the tourist potential. The gardens are open from mid-March to mid-May (daily 8–7.30), when more than 7 million bulbs are in bloom, laid out in brilliant swathes of red, yellow, pink and blue.

Shopping

ATELIER TEMPEL
ateliertempel.nl
At her studio in De Pijp neighbourhood, artist and former Oilily fashion designer Hilde Tempelma makes unique pieces of pottery, bags and scarfs, as well as items to decorate your home.
🔛 E8 ✉ Eerste Jacob van Campenstraat 20 ☎ 470 0106 🚋 Tram 16

DE BAZAAR
debazaar.nl
This huge indoor flea market, 26km (16 miles) northwest of Amsterdam, is one of Europe's largest, with more than 300 stalls, 700 shops and 70 eateries. It also has a great Middle Eastern market with all kinds of exotic goods.
🔛 Off map at A1 ✉ Montageweg 35 Beverwijk ☎ 0251 262626 🕐 Sat–Sun 8.30–6 🚉 Beverwijk-Oost

GATHERSHOP
gathershop.nl
Inside an historic former tram depot that's been turned into a cultural centre, you'll find this delicately curated shop filled with fairtrade, handmade and simple objects.
🔛 C6 ✉ Hannie Dankbaarpassage 19 ☎ 752 0681 🚋 Tram 7, 17

POL'S POTTEN
polspotten.nl
A large warehouse in the Eastern Docklands area is home to this store selling imaginative and quirky home décor items, including furniture, lamps, tableware and pottery. Most of the products you'll see here are locally designed.
🔛 M4 ✉ KNSM-laan 39 ☎ 419 3541 🚋 Tram 10

Entertainment and Nightlife

AMSTERDAM ARENA
amsterdamarena.nl
Voetbal (soccer) is Holland's number one spectator sport, and you can watch Ajax, one of the best teams in the world, play at this magnificent stadium. Concerts are also held at this 50,000-seater venue as well, but you'll need to plan ahead to get tickets.
🔛 Off map ✉ ArenA Boulevard 1, Amsterdam Zuidoost ☎ 311 1333 🚉 Strandvliet

APOLLOHAL
apollobasketball.nl
The city's professional basketball team is called BC Apollo and their home turf is the modernist 1930s' Apollohal. Catch an exciting game here or use the adjacent health and fitness club.
🔛 Off map ✉ Apollolaan 4, Amsterdam Zuid ☎ 662 9720 🚌 Bus 65

BIMHUIS
bimhuis.nl
Top local and international jazz musicians regularly grace the stage at this concert hall, which sees more than 150 shows per year. Check the website for who's playing. The café and restaurant here are worth a visit too, not just for the food but for the views.
🔛 K4 ✉ Piet Heinkade 3 ☎ 788 2150 🚋 Tram 26

CAFÉ SARPHAAT

This popular local café at the southeast corner of the Sarphatipark comes into its own in the evenings, when it serves drinks and food until 1am (3am Fri and Sat). You can indulge yourself with rich chocolate cake, enjoy a mojito or two, and on warm nights sit out on the pleasant terrace.

➕ G8 ✉ Ceintuurbaan 157-A ☎ 675 1565 🚋 Tram 3

ICE SKATING

In winter, if conditions are just right, the city's canals will freeze. Locals love to bring out their skates to enjoy these magical interludes. Skates can be rented from most sports equipment stores so you can also experience this quintessential Dutch pastime. There's also a seasonal ice rink on the Museumplein, where it's as much fun to watch as to participate in.

JAAP EDEN IJSBANEN

jaapeden.nl

Named after the famous Dutch ice-skater Jaap Eden (1873–1925), this ice rink east of Amsterdam is open from October to March. It features a 400m (1,312ft) outdoor rink, an indoor rink, a beginners' course, a climbing wall and a restaurant. Saturday night is disco skating night.

➕ M9 ✉ Radioweg 64 ☎ 0900 724 2287 🚋 Tram 9

DE MIRANDABAD

amsterdam.nl

Kids (and adults) of all ages will love this subtropical swimming pool complex with various indoor and outdoor pools, beach, palm trees, wave machines and slides. There's also a restaurant and several squash courts.

➕ Off map ✉ De Mirandalaan 9 ☎ 252 4444 🚋 Tram 4

MUZIEKGEBOUW AAN 'T IJ

muziekgebouw.nl

The innovative modern concert hall is an ocean of tinted glass on the shore of the IJ channel, east of Centraal Station. It is a major venue for contemporary classical music featuring work by John Cage, Xanakis and other pioneers, including Dutch composers.

➕ K4 ✉ Piet Heinkade 1 ☎ 788 2000 🚋 Tram 26

RAI

rai.nl

Large and modern exhibition and convention centre that hosts art fairs, trade shows, international conferences, concerts and sport events.

➕ Off map ✉ Europaplein ☎ 549 1212 🚋 Tram 4

Where to Eat

PRICES

Prices are approximate, based on a 3-course meal for one person.

€€€ over €50
€€ €25–€50
€ under €25

CAFÉ-RESTAURANT AMSTERDAM (€€)

cradam.nl

This beautiful, large open space was once a 19th-century water pumping station. The menu features Dutch as well as French and Belgian dishes. The seafood platters are excellent, and especially enjoyable served out on the terrace.

➕ D2 ⌗ Watertorenplein 6, Westerpark ☎ 682 2666 ⏰ Daily 10.30–midnight (Fri–Sat until 1am) 🚋 Tram 10

CIEL BLEU (€€€)

okura.nl

The creative French and Far East-inspired menu has earned this chic restaurant two Michelin stars. On the 23rd floor of the Hotel Okura, it also offers superb service and panoramic city views.

➕ F9 ⌗ Hotel Okura, Ferdinand Bolstraat 333, De Pijp ☎ 678 7450 ⏰ Mon–Sat 6.30–10.30pm 🚋 Tram 12

DE GOUDEN REAEL (€€)

goudenreael.nl

Making full use of its romantic waterside position, this gastropub and restaurant is to be found in a 17th-century dockside building. There's fine contemporary Dutch and French cuisine and an extensive wine list.

➕ E1 ⌗ Zandhoek 14, Westerdok ☎ 623 3883 ⏰ Mon–Thu 4pm–1am, Fri–Sat noon–3am, Sun noon–1am 🚋 Tram 3; bus 48

PENDERGAST (€€)

pendergast.nl

A taste of the American Midwest can be found at this humble smokehouse in suburban Amsterdam. Fall-off-the-bone ribs, succulent brisket, and sides like mac and cheese and baked beans are winning over the locals.

➕ C2 ⌗ Groen van Prinstererstraat 14, Staatsliedenbuurt ☎ 845 8507 ⏰ Fri–Sat 5–11, Sun, Wed–Thu 5–10 🚋 Tram 10

RESTAURANT DE KAS (€€€)

restaurantdekas.nl

The setting is a large greenhouse dating back to 1926. The food is farm-to-table and vegetable-focused, with a set menu that changes daily. Much of the organic produce featured in the dishes are grown on-site or nearby.

➕ K9 ⌗ Kamerlingh Onneslaan 3, Watergraafsmeer ☎ 462 4562 ⏰ Mon–Fri 12–2, 6.30–10, Sat 6.30–10 🚋 Tram 9

LA RIVE (€€€)

restaurantlarive.nl

This is one of the best restaurants in the city, where Chef Rogér Rassin produces excellent French-Mediterranean cooking based on seasonal delicacies. The amazing cheese selection is not to be missed.

➕ G7 ⌗ Amstel Hotel, Prof Tulpplein 1 ☎ 520 3264 ⏰ Daily 6.30pm–10pm 🚋 Tram 7, 10

VISAANDESCHELDE (€€)

visaandeschelde.nl

This popular fish restaurant has an eclectic menu of dishes from around the world. Dine in the art deco interior or out on the patio.

➕ Off map ⌗ Scheldeplein 4, Rivierenbuurt ☎ 675 1583 ⏰ Mon–Fri 12–2.30, 5.30–11, Sat 5.30–11, Sun 4–11pm 🚋 Tram 4, 12, 25

Amsterdam is probably Europe's most accessible city, and there is a range of hotels to be found, though often not enough to meet demand, so book ahead.

Where to Stay

Staying in Amsterdam

One of the great attractions of a short break in Amsterdam is that virtually any hotel you consider will be within easy walking distance of all the main attractions. Staying in a hotel on a canal is obviously one of the nicest options for the location but you will pay extra. If you want peace and quiet, the Museum District and the area near Vondelpark are good options.

Finding a Bargain

Two-fifths of Amsterdam's 60,000 hotel beds are classed as top-range properties, making problems for people looking for mid-range and budget accommodation. At peak times, such as the spring tulip season and summer, empty rooms in lower-cost hotels are about as rare as black tulips. The only answer to this problem is to reserve well ahead. Special offers may be available at other times. Many hotels lower their rates in winter, when the city is far quieter than in the mad whirl of summer.

Tips for Staying

Watch out for hidden pitfalls, such as Golden Age canal houses with four floors, steep and narrow stairways and no elevator. Most of the canalside hotels are small and only offer bed-and-breakfast. Some low-price options may not offer private bathrooms. Be wary of tranquil-looking places with a late-night café's outdoor terrace next door.

RESERVATIONS

To be sure to get the rooms you require it is essential to reserve well in advance. Hotels get fully booked months ahead, in particular those with character alongside the canals. Low season, November to March, still gets booked up, as the rates drop by around a quarter. The VVV operates a hotel reservation service centre (☎ 702 6000—there's a €15 fee per reservation, but no fee for online reservations at iamsterdam.com). If you leave finding somewhere until you arrive, the tourist offices can make on-the-spot bookings for €4 per person.

By the canal or on a street corner, hotels come in all styles and prices in Amsterdam

Budget Hotels

BICYCLE HOTEL AMSTERDAM
bicyclehotel.com

Easy on the budget, this eco-friendly hotel offers a choice of shared or private bathrooms. Continental breakfast is included and if you stay five nights or more there's free bicycle rental. This is considered a backpackers' hotel, but others are welcome.

➕ F9 ✉ Van Ostadestraat 123, De Pijp ☎ 679 3452 🚋 Tram 3, 12

HOTEL ALLURE AMSTERDAM
hotel-allure.hoteleamsterdam.net

Modern, clean and simple rooms are found on a quiet residential street. There are private bathrooms and mini fridges, and some rooms have balconies with French doors. Breakfast is available for a surcharge.

➕ H7 ✉ Sarphatistraat 117, Plantage & the East ☎ 428 3708 🚋 Tram 7, 10 🚇 Weesperplein

HOTEL ARENA
hotelarena.nl

In a grand, converted 19th-century orphanage and nursing home, the rooms here are modern, bright and spacious, and come with all the mod cons. The hotel bar is chic and the breakfast buffet is worthwhile.

➕ J7 ✉ 's-Gravesandestraat 55, Oost ☎ 850 2400 🚋 Tram 7, 10

HOTEL MUSEUMZICHT
hotelmuseumzicht.nl

A simple, no frills boutique hotel with antique furnishings and views of the Rijksmuseum. Some rooms have private bathrooms. There's a little lending library and the continental breakfast is free.

➕ D7 ✉ Jan Luijenstraat 22, Museumplein ☎ 671 2954 🚋 Tram 2, 5

HOTEL PRINSENHOF
hotelprinsenhof.com

This comfortable, quaint canalside hotel has simple rooms and private bathrooms. Breakfast is often included in the rate. Be aware that the stairs are steep and narrow (as is usual in Amsterdam's canal houses).

➕ G7 ✉ Prinsengracht 810, Grachtengordel ☎ 623 1772 🚋 Tram 4

LINDEN HOTEL
lindenhotel.nl

For good value for money, try this friendly, family-run hotel, which you'll find along a little canal in a quiet part of the city. The cosy, clean rooms are accessible by elevator and have nice private bathrooms.

➕ E3 ✉ Lindengracht 251, Jordaan ☎ 622 1460 🚋 Tram 3, 10

VONDELPARK-MUSEUM B&B

Ronald, the friendly host, will welcome you to these basic but roomy apartment-like suites in an 1879 townhouse. Breakfast can be served outside on the terrace overlooking a lovely garden at the back of the property.

➕ D7 ✉ Vossiusstraat 14 ☎ +31 624 607007 🚋 Tram 2, 5

WHERE TO STAY BUDGET HOTELS

Mid-Range Hotels

AMBASSADE HOTEL
ambassade-hotel.nl
Classic 17th-century gabled canal houses are home to a variety of tastefully decorated rooms furnished with Louis XV and Louis XVI antiques and adorned with modern art. Well-known authors are often guests here; they leave behind signed copies of their work for the library bar.
➕ E5 ✉ Herengracht 341, Grachtengordel ☎ 555 0222 🚃 Tram 1, 2, 5

AMSTERDAM
hotelamsterdam.nl
Fully modernized white rooms with soundproof windows and mini bars lie behind the Amsterdam's 18th-century facade, on one of the city's busiest tourist streets.
➕ F4 ✉ Damrak 93–94, Centrum ☎ 555 0666 🚃 Tram 4, 9, 14, 16

BILDERBERG HOTEL JAN LUYKEN
bilderberg.nl
Several elegant townhouses make up this family and pet-friendly hotel. Rooms are modern, in beige tones, and include nespresso machines. The package deals are good value.
➕ D7 ✉ Jan Luijkenstraat 58, Museumplein ☎ 573 0730 🚃 Tram 2, 3, 5, 12

CANAL HOUSE
canalhouse.nl
A 17th-century facade, spacious, modern rooms in deep hues, and gorgeous bathrooms make this a great choice. The free continental breakfast is good

and there's also a pretty courtyard garden for afternoon tea or cocktails.
➕ E4 ✉ Keizersgracht 148, Jordaan ☎ 622 5182 🚃 Tram 13, 14, 17

HOTEL ESTHERÉA
estherea.nl
The wood-panelled rooms are colourful and lush, with modern amenities including iPads, and all have balconies. A gym, a 24-hour bar and underground parking are also available.
➕ E5 ✉ Singel 303–309, Grachtengordel ☎ 624 5146 🚃 Tram 1, 2, 5

HOTEL NOT HOTEL
hotelnothotel.com
Fancy spending the night in a tram cart or hidden behind a bookcase? Rooms at this hotel in an up-and-coming neighbourhood are works of art, and completely unconventional. The hotel's Kevin Bacon Bar is open 24 hours and serves an amazing breakfast.
➕ A6 ✉ Piri Reisplein 34, Oud-West ☎ 820 4538 🚃 Tram 7, 17

HOTEL SEBASTIAN'S
hotelsebastians.nl
This boutique, canal house hotel is in a beautiful, serene part of the Jordaan. The rooms offer contemporary decor in rich hues, nespresso machines, mini bars and nice toiletries. Some rooms have canal views, others have courtyard garden views.
➕ E3 ✉ Keizersgracht 15, Jordaan ☎ 423 2342 🚇 Centraalz

LLOYD HOTEL
lloydhotel.com
Immigrants, prisoners and then artists have all called this 1920s' national monument building home. Now it's a fun, arty hotel with a gallery, library, gift

shop and a large variety of rooms, designed by artists, featuring such things as swings and grand pianos. Each room is rated from 1 to 5 stars, rather than the whole hotel having a star rating.

➕ L4 ✉ Oostelijke Handelskade 34, Oostelijke Eilanden ☎ 561 3607 🚊 Tram 10, 26

NH COLLECTION AMSTERDAM DOELEN

nh-hotels.com

On the banks of the Amstel River sits Amsterdam's oldest hotel, where Rembrandt painted *The Night Watch* in 1642. White, modern and completely renovated rooms are clean and cosy. The breakfast buffet is heavenly.

➕ F5 ✉ Nieuwe Doelenstraat 26, Centrum ☎ 554 0600 🚊 Tram 4, 9, 14, 16

NH SCHILLER

nh-hotels.com

The art deco features at this hotel have been carefully preserved, yet all the rooms are modern and some have balconies overlooking the square. Each room has a headboard featuring paintings by Dutch artist Frits Schiller, who once owned the hotel. It's a lively part of the city and the hotel's popular brasserie serves great Dutch dishes.

➕ F6 ✉ Rembrandtplein 26, Rembrandtplein ☎ 554 0700 🚊 Tram 4, 9, 14

SEVEN BRIDGES

sevenbridgeshotel.nl

The owners treat their guests like friends at this small and exquisite hotel. With its position on the city's prettiest canal, it is everyone's special bed-and-breakfast. Rooms are eclectic and decorated with antiques.

➕ F7 ✉ Reguliersgracht 31, Grachtengordel ☎ 623 1329 🚊 Tram 4

ALTERNATIVES

From a couch to a complete canal house, or even a *woonboot* (houseboat), airbnb. com has hundreds of rental options for all budgets, tastes and lengths of stay. iamsterdam.com also has a range of choices and recommendations.

SINT NICOLAAS

hotelnicolaas.nl

In the unlikely setting of a cosily converted rope factory, this hotel has welcoming rooms with dark wooden floors and quality amenities. It's great value considering the central location. Continental breakfast is included.

➕ F3 ✉ Spuistraat 1a, Centrum ☎ 626 1384 🚊 Tram 1, 2, 5, 13, 17

THE TOREN

thetoren.nl

The Toren is in two beautifully converted canal houses, one of which used to be a safe house during World War II. Each room is romantically decorated in sumptuously dark furnishings. Nespresso machines, mini bar and bathrobes are just some of the luxe touches. The elegant breakfast buffet is certainly recommended.

➕ E4 ✉ Keizersgracht 164, Jordaan ☎ 622 63 52 🚊 Tram 13, 14, 17

VONDEL

hotelvondel.com

This boutique hotel is situated on a quiet residential street near Vondelpark. The rooms are all stylish and individually designed, and some have balconies and hot tubs. The large courtyard garden is wonderful, and the restaurant is next door.

➕ D7 ✉ Vondelstraat 26, Oud West ☎ 612 0120 🚊 Tram 1, 6

Luxury Hotels

PRICES

Expect to pay over €250 per night for a double room in a luxury hotel.

BANKS MANSION

carlton.nl

The art deco features add to the style of this hotel in a former bank. The rate includes drinks and snacks in the hotel bar and a breakfast buffet. Other amenities include rain showers, nespresso machines and iPads.

🚹 F6 ✉ Herengracht 519–525 ☎ 420 0055 🚊 Tram 16

THE DYLAN

dylanamsterdam.com

The conversion of this 17th-century building is stunning. The lavish, high-end rooms have been individually themed. The hotel's restaurant is Michelin-starred Vinkeles (▷ 36).

🚹 E5 ✉ Keizersgracht 384, Grachtengordel ☎ 530 2010 🚊 Tram 1, 2, 5

DE L'EUROPE

deleurope.com

Marble bathrooms, private balconies and Amstel River views are just some of the perks at this grande dame marvel. The hotel's Michelin-starred restaurant Bord'Eau (▷ 60) is fantastic.

🚹 F5 ✉ Nieuwe Doelenstraat 2–14, Centrum ☎ 531 1777 🚊 Tram 4, 9, 14, 16

HAMPSHIRE HOTEL AMSTERDAM AMERICAN

hampshirehotelamsterdamamerican.com

This grand, art nouveau hotel on a busy square has spacious, contemporary rooms with balconies. Enjoy afternoon tea or fine Dutch cuisine on the terrace.

🚹 D6 ✉ Leidsekade 97, Grachtengordel ☎ 556 3000 🚊 Tram 1, 2, 5, 6, 7, 10

INTERCONTINENTAL AMSTEL

amsterdam.intercontinental.com

Celebrities choose to stay at this graceful and ultra-luxurious hotel on the Amstel River. Antique-filled rooms come with marble bathrooms, and the hotel has an indoor pool, spa and one of the city's best restaurants, La Rive (▷ 106).

🚹 G7 ✉ Prof Tulpplein 1, Amstel ☎ 622 6060 🚇 Weesperplein 🚊 Tram 6, 7, 10

NH GRAND HOTEL KRASNAPOLSKY

nh-hotels.com

Built in 1855, the "Kras" has belle époque grace in its public spaces and luxurious modern rooms. The Winter Garden atrium, where breakfast is served, is simply stunning.

🚹 F4 ✉ Dam 9, Centrum ☎ 554 9111 🚊 Tram 4, 9, 14, 16

PULITZER

pulitzeramsterdam.com

Twenty-five 17th- and 18th-century houses have been converted into this luxurious canalside hotel. Split levels and wooden beams retain an authentic Dutch ambience. The hotel's boat is available for tours.

🚹 E5 ✉ Prinsengracht 315–331, Grachtengordel ☎ 523 5235 🚊 Tram 13, 14, 17

SOFITEL LEGEND THE GRAND AMSTERDAM

sofitel.com

Previously a 16th-century monastery, royal inn and the City Hall, the Grand is now a luxury hotel with vivid colour schemes, modern rooms and full amenities. French restaurant Bridges (▷ 61) is worth a visit.

🚹 F5 ✉ Oudezijds Voorburgwal 197, Centrum ☎ 555 3111 🚇 Nieuwmarkt

Readily accessible by plane, boat and train, Amsterdam has the added bonus of having excellent public transportation and is easy to walk around.

Planning Ahead

When to Go

Most tourists visit Amsterdam between April and September; late March to late May is the time to see tulips in bloom. June brings the Holland Festival of art, dance, opera and plays. Although winter can be cold and damp, December is crowded with Christmas shoppers and those staying for the festive season.

AVERAGE DAILY MAXIMUM TEMPERATURES

JAN	FEB	MAR	APR	MAY	JUN	JUL	AUG	SEP	OCT	NOV	DEC
41°F	43°F	48°F	55°F	63°F	68°F	72°F	72°F	68°F	57°F	46°F	41°F
5°C	6°C	9°C	13°C	17°C	20°C	22°C	22°C	20°C	14°C	8°C	5°C

Spring (March to May) is at its most delightful in May—with the least rainfall and the crowds not so intense as the summer months.
Summer (June to August) is the sunniest time of year but good weather is not guaranteed.
Autumn (September to November) gets wetter, although September is a popular time to visit. The weather is often chilly and drizzly as winter approaches.
Winter (December to February) can be cold, and temperatures can drop so low that the canals freeze. Strong winds can increase the chill factor, and fog can blot out the sunlight for days.

WHAT'S ON

January *National Tulip Day.*
January/February *Chinese New Year* in Chinatown.
February/March *Carnival.*
March *Stille Omgang* (2nd Sat night): Silent procession.
April *National Museum Week*: Museums lower entrance fees; *Koningsdag* (27 Apr): The King's official birthday.
May *Remembrance Day* (4 May): Pays tribute to World War II victims; *Liberation Day* (5 May): Marking the end of the German Occupation in 1945.

National Windmill Day (2nd Sat); *National Cycling Day* (2nd Sun).
June *Holland Festival*: International arts festival; *Amsterdam Roots Festival*: ethnic cultural festival
July *Over Het IJ Festival* (early Jul): contemporary theatre, music and dance at the NDSM-Werf.
August *Amsterdam Gay Pride* (early Aug): one of Europe's biggest gay festivals; *Grachtenfestival* (mid-Aug): annual canal festival, with the *Prinsengracht-concert*,

music recitals on barges outside the Hotel Pulitzer; *Jordaan Festival* (late Aug): street party
September *Amsterdam Heritage Day* (2nd Sat): Buildings open to the public, with free admission.
November *Sinterklaas* (mid-Nov): Procession with Sinterklaas and Zwarte Piet.
December *Oudejaarsavond* (31 Dec): Street parties, fireworks; *Amsterdam Light Festival* (early Dec to mid Jan): large scale light installations across the city.

Amsterdam Online
amsterdam.info
hotels.nl
Accommodation sites: The first site represents a cross-section of hotels in the city, from budget to deluxe, including apartments and houseboats. The second covers the whole of the Netherlands, and is useful if you want to travel farther afield or find hotels in nearby towns when all the hotels in Amsterdam are full. Both sites have up-to-date details of tariffs, special offers and room availability, with pictures of typical rooms on offer and maps showing the precise location.

iamsterdam.com
holland.com
Official tourist board sites: The first covers Amsterdam and the second the whole of the Netherlands. They are good for information about exhibitions, events and festivals. Both have online hotel booking.

awesomeamsterdam.com
Run by ex-pats and locals permanently living in Amsterdam, this site covers the latest attractions, restaurants, bars and events. It also has useful cultural information and great tips for visitors.

dinnersite.nl
Say what kind of food you like and you'll get a comprehensive list of Amsterdam restaurants to suit. More than 10,000 restaurants are featured on this site, covering all the Netherlands, and you can specify criteria such as "child friendly" or "wheelchair accessible". You can also use the site to make reservations online.

amsterdam.nl
This is the official site of the city of Amsterdam. It's mainly aimed at locals but you can find information on living and working in the city, its neighbourhoods, parks, buildings, heritage sites and more.

TRAVEL SITES

fodors.com
A complete travel-planning site. You can research prices and weather; book air tickets, cars and rooms; pose questions (and get answers) to fellow visitors; and find links to other sites.
eurostar.com
For details of international rail services.
ns.nl
Journey planner for getting around Holland by train.

WIFI

The Netherlands has one of the fastest internet speeds in the world. Most hotels, restaurants, cafés and museums readily offer free WiFi. Grocery store chains such as Albert Heijn and Marqt offer it too, as does Schiphol airport.

Getting There

VISAS AND TRAVEL INSURANCE

Citizens of the US, UK, Ireland, Canada, New Zealand and Australia do not need a visa to enter the Netherlands if staying for three months or less. You do need a passport, a return air ticket and sufficient funds to cover the cost of your visit, though in practice these are seldom checked. Always check the Government of the Netherlands website (government.nl) for updated entry requirements. EU citizens can obtain health care with the production of the EHIC card. However, insurance to cover illness and theft is strongly advised.

DRIVING

Follow the excellent signage for parking as you come into the city but be aware that provision often falls short of demand. The scarcity and high cost of parking, combined with the one-way, narrow streets and the large number of cyclists mean that driving is not an ideal way of getting about the city. Cars are generally discouraged and any penalties incurred will be high. During the annual King's Day celebrations around 27 April, many city roads are closed to traffic. Never drive under the influence of alcohol.

AIRPORTS

There are direct international flights into Schiphol Airport from around the world, as well as good rail connections with most European cities and regular sailings from the UK to major ferry ports, all of which have good rail connections to Amsterdam.

60km (40 miles)

IJmuiden ferry
50 min,
€6

Schiphol Airport
20 min,
€5.20

Rotterdam ferry
1 hr,
€15

Hoek van Holland ferry
Train 1 hr 35 min,
€18

FROM SCHIPHOL

Schiphol (tel 794 0800, schiphol.nl), Amsterdam's only international airport, is 18km (11 miles) southwest of the heart of the city. Many international airlines operate scheduled and charter flights here. Trains leave the airport for Amsterdam Centraal Station every 10 minutes from 6am until midnight, then hourly through the night. The ride takes 20 minutes and costs €5.20. Connexxion Schiphol Hotel Shuttle buses run from the airport to most hotels and you can request a hotel if it is not on the list. The cost is €17 one-way, €27 return; 6am–9.30pm (tel 038 339 4741, schiphol-hotelshuttle.nl). You should never have to wait more than 30 minutes for a bus and they can be every 10 minutes. It leaves outside Arrivals 2 at platform A7. Taxis are available but fares run as high as €50. It is faster to go by train to Centraal Station and take a taxi from there.

ARRIVING BY RAIL

Centraal Station has direct connections from major cities in western Europe, including high-speed links from Paris, Brussels and Cologne.

From Britain, there are connections at Brussels with trains operated by Eurostar, with bargain through fares to Amsterdam. For general train information call 751 5155 or visit ns.nl.

CENTRAAL STATION

Whether you come from the airport or the ferry port, or on an international train, you will end up at this station (▷ 51). A few tips can help you avoid problems on arrival:

● Once off the platforms the main concourse is crowded with people.

● The station is a magnet for pickpockets and hustlers who target tourists.

● Heading out of the main entrance you will be confronted with a confusion of taxis, trams, buses and bicycles.

● The main taxi rank is to the right of the main entrance as are the following tram stands: 1, 2, 5, 13 and 17.

● To the left are tram stands 4, 9, 16 and 26, and the entrance to the Metro.

● Just beyond is the city's main tourist office (VVV) in a white building.

● To the left is the GVB Tickets & Info public transportation office, where you buy travel passes and reserve tickets for canal cruises (open Mon–Fri 7am–9pm, Sat–Sun 8am–6pm).

● Water transportation options are the Canal Bus, the Hop On-Hop Off boats, Water Taxi, canal-boat tours, and, at the rear of the station, passenger ferries and two-wheel transportation to three different points on the north bank of Het IJ.

ARRIVING BY SEA

The major ferry ports—IJmuiden (23km/14 miles), Rotterdam Europoort (70km/43 miles) and Hoek van Holland (Hook of Holland, 68km/42 miles)—have good rail connections with Amsterdam. Regular sailings from the UK are offered by Stena Line (stenaline.co.uk), DFDS Seaways (dfdsseaways.co.uk) and P&O Ferries (poferries.com).

CUSTOMS

Allowances (17 years up)
Goods Bought Outside the EU (Duty-Free Limits):
Alcohol: 1 litre of spirits over 22% volume, OR 2 litres of fortified wine, sparkling wine or other liqueurs, PLUS 4 litres of still table wine
Tobacco: 200 cigarettes, OR 100 cigarillos, OR 50 cigars, OR 250g of tobacco
Perfume: 50ml
Toilet water: 250ml

Goods Bought Inside the EU for Your Own Use (Guidance Levels):
Alcohol: 10 litres of spirits AND 20 litres of fortified wine, sparkling wine or other liqueurs, AND 90 litres of wine, AND 110 litres of beer
Tobacco: 800 cigarettes, AND 400 cigarillos, AND 200 cigars, AND 1kg of tobacco

Not allowed:
Drugs, firearms, ammunition, offensive weapons, obscene material, unlicensed animals including birds and insects

CAR RENTAL

You will find the usual leading international rental companies both at Schiphol Airport and in the city.

Getting Around

ACCESSIBILITY

The Netherlands is one of the most progressive countries in the world when it comes to providing access and information. Hotels, museums and buildings that meet minimum standards display the International Accessibility Symbol. Tourist Information Offices have full information on hotels, restaurants, museums, tourist attractions and boat and bus excursions with facilities for people with disabilities. Wheelchair accessible taxis can be ordered through TCA (☎ 777 7777; tcataxi.nl). For further information visit clientenbelangamsterdam.nl.

CANAL TRAVEL

You can buy an all-day ticket for the Canal Bus although the route and schedules are not too easy to follow. Water taxis have to be reserved in advance and are expensive. See panel opposite for more details.

HOP ON-HOP OFF

Hop On-Hop Off Amsterdam (citysightseeingamsterdam. nl) runs buses and boats along routes for all the major attractions, so you can combine sightseeing with getting around. Tickets are valid for 24 or 48 hours.

TRAMS AND BUSES

● Fourteen different tram lines have frequent services from 6am on weekdays (slightly later at weekends) until 12.15am. In addition, there are dozens of city (GVB) and regional (Arriva and Connexxion) bus services. A service of 12 night bus lines operates in the city from about 12.30am to about 6.30am. Day tickets are valid during the night following the day on which they were issued.

● It is best to buy your ticket in advance but for a single journey you can pay the conductor. Take care when getting off; many stops are in the middle of the road. For maps and timetables, and much more city public transportation information, go to gvb.nl.

METRO

● There are four Metro lines, three terminating at Centraal Station, used mainly by commuters from the suburbs.

● The most useful city stations are Centraal Station, Nieuwmarkt and Waterlooplein.

TAXIS

● Taxis are plentiful, though not used as often as in most other cities because of the nature of Amsterdam's streets and canals. Traffic easily becomes congested, and it can be quicker to walk, cycle or take public transportation. Taxi fares are quite high.

● You can call a taxi by ringing the main city taxi company, TCA (tel 777 7777). There is a taxi rank outside Centraal Station, and a few others around the city, including at Leidseplein and Rembrandtplein, and you can also hail a cab on the streets.

TICKETS

● Like all other *openbaar vervoer* (public transportation) companies in the Netherlands, GVB Amsterdam uses the OV-chipkaart (chipcard) as a way of paying for using the city's Metro, tram and bus services (and NS/Dutch Railways trains).

• The OV-chipkaart is a smart card that you swipe when entering and leaving the public transport system; the cost of your journey is calculated and deducted from the balance on the card. The basic cost of the card (▷ below) is non-refundable. You also have to pay a fee to recover any unused balance.

• Three main types of OV-chipkaart are available: a reloadable "personal" card (€7.50 for the card plus up to €150 worth of travel) that can be used only by the person whose picture is on the card; a reloadable "anonymous" card (€7.50 for the card plus up to €150 worth of travel), which can be used by anyone; and, for limited use, "throwaway" cards (€2.50 and €4.80), which, unlike the other two cards, can only be used with the company of purchase.

• Electronic readers at Metro and train stations, and on trams and buses, deduct the fare, which is calculated per kilometre.

• GVB Amsterdam day and multi-day cards—which function like chipcards—may be simpler and more cost-effective for visitors making frequent use of the city's public transportation. These cards cost: 24 hours (€7.50), 48 hours (€12.50), 72 hours (€17), 96 hours (€22), 120 hours (€27), 144 hours (€31), 168 hours (€34).

• Buy OV-chipkaart and other cards from GVB Tickets & Info and Metro stations.

• Don't travel without a valid ticket, as you will be fined €35 on the spot.

• For further information and maps, contact GVB Tickets & Info at Stationsplein (tel 0900 8011, gvb.nl).

GETTING AROUND BY BICYCLE

• The best way to see Amsterdam is by bicycle. There are plenty of cycle lanes, distances are short and there are no hills.

• To rent a bike costs from €10 a day, €40 a week: Damstraat Rent-a-Bike (Damstraat 20–22, tel 625 5029, rentabike.nl, open daily 9–6); Bike City (Bloemgracht 68–70, tel 626 3721, bikecity.nl, open daily 9–6).

ORGANIZED SIGHTSEEING

Canal boats are not a part of the public transportation system and although quite expensive are a wonderful way to see the city. The busiest canal-boat docks are those at Centraal Station and on nearby Damrak. Other docks around the city are Rokin, Leidseplein and Stadhouderskade (at Ferdinand Bolstraat).

Rederij Kooij
☎ 623 3810; rederijkooij.nl.
Daily city cruises from 10–10 in the summer and till 5pm in the winter.

Stromma Netherlands
☎ 217 0501; stromma.nl
Water-bus service around the city. Hop On-Hop Off day pass is a good option.

Lovers
☎ 530 1090; lovers.nl
Tours daily 9–6, every 30 min.

Blue Boat Canal Cruises
☎ 679 1370; blueboat.nl
Daily city cruises from 10–6.

Other options
Yellow Bike Tours
✉ Nieuwezijds Kolk 29
☎ 620 6940;
yellowbike.nl

Mee in Mokum walking tours
✉ Keizersgracht 346
☎ 625 1390;
meeinmokum.nl
Tours Tue–Sun 11 and 2

Essential Facts

The euro is the official currency of the Netherlands. Bank notes are in denominations of 5, 10, 20, 50, 100, 200 and 500 euros and coins in denominations of 1, 2, 5, 10, 20 and 50 cents and 1 and 2 euros.

EXCHANGE RATES

Banks may offer a better exchange rate than hotels or independent bureaux de change. GWK Travelex (Geldswisselkantoor) offer money-changing services at Schiphol Airport and at Centraal Station and in many locations around the city.

ELECTRICITY

● 230 volts; round two-pin sockets.

MEDICINES

● For nonprescription drugs, and so on, go to a *drogist*. For prescription medicines, go to an *apotheek;* most open Mon–Fri 8.30–5.30.

● Details of pharmacies open outside normal hours are in the daily newspaper *Het Parool* and all pharmacy windows.

● Outside normal working hours, for an emergency doctor's office that operates 24 hours, even on public holidays, call 088 003 0600.

● Hospital *(ziekenhuis)* outpatient clinics are open 24 hours. The most central is Onze-Lieve-Vrouwe Gasthuis at Oosterpark 9 (tel 599 9111, olvg.nl).

NATIONAL HOLIDAYS

● 1 January; Good Friday, Easter Sunday and Monday; 27 April; Ascension Day; Pentecost Sunday and Monday; 25 and 26 December. Many attractions are closed on some or all of these days.

● 4 and 5 May—Remembrance Day *(Herdenkingsdag)* and Liberation Day *(Bevrijdingsdag)*—are both World War II commemoration days.

NEWSPAPERS AND MAGAZINES

● The main Dutch newspapers are *De Telegraaf* (right wing), *De Volkskrant* (left wing) and *NRC Handelsblad.*

● The main Amsterdam paper is *Het Parool.*

● Listings magazines: *Amsterdam Day by Day, A-mag* (published six times per year) and *Uitkrant* (monthly).

● Foreign newspapers are widely available.

OPENING HOURS

● Banks: Mon–Fri 9 until 4 or 5. Some stay open Thu until 7.

● Shops: Tue–Sat 9 or 10 until 6, Mon 1 to 6. Some open Thu until 9 and Sun noon until 5. Some close early Sat, at 4 or 5.

● State-run museums and galleries: most open Tue–Sat 10 to 5, Sun and national holidays 1 to 5. Many close on Mon.

POST OFFICES
● Most post offices open Mon–Fri 8.30 or 9–5.
● The main Post Office is PostNL Postkantoor at Singel 250 (tel 330 0555, open Mon–Fri 8–6.30, Sat 9–5).
● For postal information check postnl.nl.
● Purchase stamps (postzegels) at post offices, tobacconists and souvenir shops.
● Post boxes are orange.
● For overseas mail use the overige bestemmingen slot.

SENSIBLE PRECAUTIONS
● As in any major city, pickpockets usually operate in busy shopping streets and markets, and in the Red Light District, so be on your guard.
● At night, avoid poorly lit areas and keep to busy streets.
● If you are travelling alone, public transportation is generally busy even late at night. A rented bicycle (or a taxi) can remove the need to use infrequent night buses or walk alone in quiet or deserted areas.

STUDENTS
For discounts at some museums, galleries, restaurants and hotels, students under 30 can obtain a Cultural Youth Passport (CJP— Cultureel Jongeren Paspoort), costing €17.50 from cjp.nl.

TELEPHONES
● Of the few public telephones that are left, most take phonecards available from telephone hubs, post offices, rail stations and newsagents.
● For national directory enquiries, call 0900 8008, and for international directory enquiries, call 0900 8418
● Numbers starting 0900 are premium rate; 0800 are free; 06 are mobile phone numbers.
● For the operator, call 0800 0410.

LOST PROPERTY
● For insurance purposes, report lost or stolen property to the police as soon as possible.
● Main lost property offices: Centraal Station
⊞ G3 ✉ Stationsplein 15
☎ 557 8544 ⏰ Daily 8–8
● Police Lost Property
⊞ E6 ✉ Korte Leidsedwarsstraat 52
☎ 251 0222
⏰ Mon–Fri 9–4
● For property lost on public transport, GVB ⊞ Off map, west of A2 ✉ Arlandaweg 100 ☎ 0900 8011
⏰ Mon–Fri 9–4

NEED TO KNOW ESSENTIAL FACTS

I AMSTERDAM CITY CARD

The best way to save on attractions in Amsterdam is through this smart card. Over 50 free and 60 discounted offers are included, plus unlimited use of GVB public transportation in the city, a free canal cruise, a city map, and more. Attractions include the Van Gogh Museum, Stedelijk Museum, Artis, NEMO Science Museum and many more. Prices start at €57 euro for a 24-hour card. Order your card online ahead of your visit at iamsterdam.com.

● To phone abroad, dial 00 then the country code (UK 44, US and Canada 1, Australia 61, New Zealand 64, Ireland 353, South Africa 27), then the number.
● Most hotels have international direct dialling, but it is expensive.
● The code for Amsterdam is 020. To phone from outside Holland drop the first 0.

TOILETS
● There are few public toilets. Use facilities in museums, department stores and the bigger hotels. There is often a small charge (€0.30–€0.50).

TOURIST OFFICES (VVV)
● Staff at the two visitor information centres (VVV) can make reservations for a small fee. You can also purchase the I amsterdam City Card there (see panel). The offices are at: Stationsplein 10 (across from Centraal Station), and Schiphol Airport Arrivals 2 at Schiphol Plaza (tel 702 6000, iamsterdam.com).

EMERGENCY PHONE NUMBERS

Police, ambulance, fire	☎ 112
Amsterdam Doctors Service	☎ 088 003 0600
Automobile Emergency (ANWB)	☎ 088 269 2888
Lost credit cards	American Express ☎ 0800 528 4800
	Diners Club ☎ 0800 234 6377
	Master/Eurocard ☎ 0800 424 7787
	Visa ☎ 0800 022 3110
Victim Support	☎ 0900 0101
Crisis Helpline	☎ 675 7575

EMBASSIES AND CONSULATES

American Consulate	✉ Museumplein 19 ☎ 575 5309
Australian Embassy	✉ Carnegielean 4a, The Hague ☎ 070 310 8200
British Consulate	✉ Koningslaan 44 ☎ 676 4343
Canadian Embassy	✉ Sophialaan 7, The Hague ☎ 070 311 1600
Irish Embassy	✉ Scheveningseweg 112, The Hague ☎ 070 363 0993
New Zealand Embassy	✉ Eisenhowerlaan 77, The Hague ☎ 070 346 9324
South African Embassy	✉ Wassenaarseweg 36, The Hague ☎ 070 392 4501

Language

BASICS

ja	yes
nee	no
alstublieft	please
bedankt	thank you
hallo	hello
goedemorgen	good morning
goedemiddag	good afternoon
goedenavond	good evening
welterusten	goodnight
dag	goodbye

USEFUL WORDS

goed/slecht	good/bad
groot/klein	big/small
warm/koud	hot/cold
nieuw/oud	new/old
open/gesloten	open/closed
ingang/uitgang	entrance/exit
heren/damen	men's/women's
wc	lavatory
vrij/bezet	free/occupied
ver/dichtbij	far/near
links/rechts	left/right
rechtdoor	straight ahead

NUMBERS

een	1
twee	2
drie	3
vier	4
vijf	5
zes	6
zeven	7
acht	8
negen	9
tien	10
elf	11
twaalf	12
dertien	13
veertien	14
vijftien	15
zestien	16
zeventien	17
achttien	18
negentien	19
twintig	20
dertig	30
veertig	40
vijftig	50
honderd	100
duizend	1,000

USEFUL PHRASES

Spreekt u engels?	Do you speak English?
Zijn er nog kamers vrij?	Do you have a vacant room?
met bad/douche	with bath/shower
Ik versta u niet	I don't understand
Waar is/zijn?	Where is/are …?
Hoe ver is het naar?	How far is it to …?
Hoeveel kost dit? …	How much does this cost?
Hoe laat gaat u open?	What time do you open?
Hoe laat gaat u dicht?	What time do you close?
Kunt u mij helpen?	Can you help me?

DAYS AND TIMES

Zondag	Sunday
Maandag	Monday
Dinsdag	Tuesday
Woensdag	Wednesday
Donderdag	Thursday
Vrijdag	Friday
Zaterdag	Saturday
vandaag	today
gisteren	yesterday
morgen	tomorrow

Timeline

Herring fishermen settle on the Amstel in the 13th century and a dam is built across the river. In 1300, the settlement is given city status and in 1345 becomes an important pilgrimage place and a major trading post, although remaining very small.

If there had been no herring, Amsterdam might never have come into existence. In the Middle Ages, the Dutch discovered how to cure these fish, and they became a staple food. Herring fishermen built a dam across the Amstel River and a small fishing village developed, Amstelledamme. Its site is now the Dam, Amsterdam's main square.

1425 First horseshoe canal, the Singel, is dug.

1517 Protestant Reformation in Germany. In subsequent decades Lutheran and Calvinist ideas take root in the city.

1519 Amsterdam becomes part of the Spanish empire and nominally Catholic.

1567–68 Start of the Eighty Years' War against Spanish rule.

1578 Amsterdam capitulates to William of Orange. Calvinists take power.

17th century Dutch Golden Age. Amsterdam becomes the most important port in the world.

1613 Work starts on the Gratchtengordel (Canal Ring).

1642 Rembrandt paints his classic work *The Night Watch*.

1648 End of war with Spain.

1652–54 First of a series of wars with Britain for maritime supremacy.

1806 Napoleon takes over the republic.

1813 Prince William returns from exile. Crowned William I in 1814.

1876 North Sea Canal opens, bringing new prosperity.

1914–18 World War I. The Netherlands is neutral.

1919 KLM Royal Dutch Airlines is founded.

1928 Amsterdam hosts the Olympics.

1940–45 German Occupation in World War II. Anne Frank goes into hiding.

1960s–70s Hippies flock to the city from around Europe.

1980 Queen Beatrix crowned. The city is named Holland's capital.

1989 New laws aim to eventually free the city of traffic.

1990 Van Gogh centenary exhibition attracts 890,000 visitors.

2013 Queen Beatrix abdicates and her son Willem-Alexander becomes Europe's youngest monarch at the age of 46.

2016 Rare Anne Frank poem, penned in March 1942, fetches €140,000 at auction.

2017 The Netherlands is the first country to use wind energy to power all of its electric trains.

A POPULAR MONARCH

Beatrix, former Queen of the Netherlands, came to the throne when her mother, Queen Juliana, abdicated on 30 April 1980. Beatrix, born in 1938, was inaugurated at the Nieuwe Kerk. Her great popularity was reflected on her official birthday (*Koninginnedag*, 30 April)—an exuberantly celebrated national holiday. This is now *Koningsdag*, King's Day, and is celebrated on 27 April, King Willem-Alexander's birthday.

From far left: Napoleon Bonaparte; ornate ceramic panel with portrait of artist Frans Hals; waiting outside the Anne Frank House; statue of Rembrandt; Neptune at the Amsterdam Maritime Museum

Index

Amsterdam 25 Best

WRITTEN BY Teresa Fisher
ADDITIONAL WRITING Hilary Weston and Jackie Staddon
UPDATED BY Lisa Voormeij
SERIES EDITOR Clare Ashton
COVER DESIGN Chie Ushio, Yuko Inagaki
DESIGN WORK Liz Baldin
IMAGE RETOUCHING AND REPRO Ian Little

Published in the United Kingdom by AA Publishing

ISBN 978-0-1475-4702-6

TENTH EDITION

All details in this book are based on information supplied to us at press time. Always confirm information when it matters, especially if you're making a detour to visit a specific place. Fodor's expressly disclaims any liability, loss, or risk, personal or otherwise, that is incurred as a consequence of the use of any of the contents of this book.

SPECIAL SALES
This book is available for special discounts for bulk purchases for sales promotions or premiums. For more information, email specialmarkets@penguinrandomhouse.com.

Color separation by AA Digital Department
Printed and bound by Leo Paper Products, China

10 9 8 7 6 5 4 3 2 1

A05522
Maps in this title produced from mapping © MAIRDUMONT / Falk Verlag 2015
Transport map © Communicarta Ltd, UK

The Automobile Association would like to thank the following photographers, companies and picture libraries for their assistance in the preparation of this book.

2 AA/M Jourdan; 3 AA/Jourdan; 4t AA/M Jourdan; 4c NBTC; 5t AA/M Jourdan; 5c NBTC; 6t AA/M Jourdan; 6cl AA/A Kouprianoff; 6cr AA/A Kouprianoff; 6bl AA/A Kouprianoff; 6br AA/A Kouprianoff; 7t AA/M Jourdan; 7cl NBTC; 7cr NBTC; 7bl NBTC; 7bc AA/M Jourdan; 7br AA/M Jourdan; 8 AA/M Jourdan; 9 AA/M Jourdan; 10t AA/M Jourdan; 10ct NBTC; 10c NBTC; 10cb NBTC; 10b NBTC; 11t AA/M Jourdan; 11ct NBTC; 11c NBTC; 11cb NBTC; 11b NBTC; 12 AA/M Jourdan; 13t AA/M Jourdan; 13ct NBTC; 13c AA/A Kouprianoff; 13cb Digital Vision; 13b NBTC; 14t AA/M Jourdan; 14ct AA/M Jourdan; 14c Hotel Dylan, Vinkeles; 14cb Visaandeschelde; 14b Hotel Okura, Ciel Bleu Restaurant; 15 AA/M Jourdan; 16t AA/M Jourdan; 16ct Delft; 16cb AA/K Paterson; 16b NBTC; 17t AA/M Jourdan; 17ct AA/K Paterson; 17c AA/A Kouprianoff; 17cb AA/K Paterson; 17b NBTC; 18t AA/M Jourdan; 18ct Hotel Dylan; 18c NBTC; 18cb NBTC; 18b AA/M Jourdan; 19t AA/A Kouprianoff; 19ct AA/A Kouprianoff; 19c AA/M Jourdan; 19cb AA/K Paterson; 19b AA/M Jourdan; 20/21 AA/K Paterson; 24tl © Anne Frank House/Photographer Cris Toala Olivares; 24bl © Anne Frank House; 24/25 Anne Frank House (photographer Allard Bovenberg); 25 Anne Frank House (photographers Allard Bovenberg); 26l AA/K Paterson; 27l NBTC; 27r NBTC; 28 Houseboat Museum, Amsterdam; 29t NBTC; 29bl AA/M Jourdan; 30t NBTC; 30b AA/A Kouprianoff; 31 AA/K Paterson; 32 AA/K Paterson; 33 AA/K Paterson; 34 AA/K Paterson; 35 AA/A Kouprianoff; 36 AA/A Kouprianoff; 37 NBTC; 40l AA/M Jourdan; 40/41 NBTC; 40/41tl NBTC; 40/41b AA/K Paterson; 41t AA/K Paterson; 41r AA/K Paterson; 42 NBTC; 43l AA/M Jourdan; 43r AA/K Paterson; 44l AA/K Paterson; 44r NBTC; 45l NBTC; 45r AA/K Paterson; 46l AA/K Paterson; 46r NBTC; 47l Hemis/Alamy Stock Photo; 48l AA/M Jourdan; 48r NBTC; 49 NBTC; 50l AA/K Paterson; 50r AA/K Paterson; 51t NBTC; 51b NBTC; 52t NBTC; 52bl AA/A Kouprianoff; 52br AA/K Paterson; 53t NBTC; 53b AA/M Jourdan; 54 AA/K Paterson; 55 AA/M Jourdan; 56 AA/M Jourdan; 57 AA/M Jourdan; 58 AA/M Jourdan; 58c Photodisc; 59 Photodisc; 60t Photodisc; 60c AA/A Kouprianoff; 61 AA/A Kouprianoff; 62 AA/A Kouprianoff; 63 AA/A Kouprianoff; 64 AA/A Kouprianoff; 65 NBTC; 68l Jewish Historical Museum (on loan from NIHS, Amsterdam); 68r Jewish Historical Museum (Photo: Liselore Kamping); 69l AA/K Paterson; 69r NBTC; 70l AA/M Jourdan; 70r AA/K Paterson; 71l AA/M Jourdan; 71r AA/M Jourdan; 72tl NBTC; 72cl NBTC; 73 NBTC; 72cl NBTC; 74 AA/Alex Robinson; 75t NBTC; 75b NBTC; 76t NBTC; 76bl AA/Alex Robinson; 77t NBTC; 77bl AA/K Paterson; 77br AA/K Paterson; 78 NBTC; 79t NBTC; 80 AA/K Paterson; 81 Stedelijk Museum John Lewis Marshall; 84 AA/A Kouprianoff; 85l NBTC; 85r NBTC; 86l Stedelijk Museum John Lewis Marshall; 86r © Karel Appel Foundation; 87l NBTC; 87r NBTC; 88/89 AA/M Jourdan; 89 AA/M Jourdan; 90t NBTC; 90b AA/K Paterson; 90br AA/K Paterson; 91 AA/K Paterson; 92t AA/K Paterson; 93 Digital Vision; 94 Imagestate; 95 AA/A Robinson; 98l AA/M Jourdan; 98r AA/A Kouprianoff; 99t NBTC; 99b NBTC; 100t NBTC; 100b Artis Amsterdam Royal Zoo/Ronald van Weeren; 101t NBTC; 101bl NBTC; 101br AA/M Jourdan; 102t AA/M Jourdan; 103 AA/M Jourdan; 104t Photodisc; 104c AA/T Souter; 105 AA/T Souter; 106 AA/C Sawyer; 107 AA/A Kouprianoff; 108t AA/C Sawyer; 108ct Pulitzer, Amsterdam; 108c AA/C Sawyer; 108cb AA/S McBride; 108b AA/A Kouprianoff; 109 AA/C Sawyer; 110 AA/C Sawyer; 111 AA/C Sawyer; 112 AA/C Sawyer; 113 AA/K Paterson; 114 AA/K Paterson; 115 AA/K Paterson; 116 AA/K Paterson; 117 AA/K Paterson; 118 AA/K Paterson; 119 AA/K Paterson; 120t AA/K Paterson; 121t AA/K Paterson; 121b AA/W Voysey; 122 AA/K Paterson; 123 AA/K Paterson; 124t AA/K Paterson; 124bl AA; 124bc AA/K Paterson; 124/125 AA/K Paterson; 125t AA/K Paterson; 125bc AA/A Kouprianoff; 125br AA/K Paterson

Titles in the Series